AN ORDINARY PERSON'S GUIDE TO EMPIRE

ARUNDHATI ROY

PRAISE FOR ARUNDHATI ROY'S ESSAYS

In her *Ordinary Person's Guide,* Roy's perfect pitch and sharp scalpel are, once again, a wonder and a joy to behold. No less remarkable is the range of material subjected to her sure and easy touch, and the surprising information she reveals at every turn. Another outstanding contribution.

　　—Noam Chomsky

Arundhati Roy combines brilliant reportage with a passionate, no-holds-barred commentary. I salute both her courage and her skill.

　　—Salman Rushdie

I don't know how Roy comes up with her killer one-liners, but I'm grateful. Each one is a gift, capable of transforming fear and confusion into courage and conviction.

　　—Naomi Klein

Big events seen from the keyhole of daily life. Arundhati Roy has an exceptional talent to turn facts, names, and even numbers into flesh and land. A book to be read? A breathing to be felt.

　　—Eduardo Galeano

Arundhati Roy combines her brilliant style as a novelist with her powerful commitment to social justice in producing these eloquent, penetrating essays.

—Howard Zinn

W.B. Yeats wrote that "the best lack all conviction, while the worst are full of passionate intensity," but Roy is an exception. She overflows with Passionate Conviction. No wonder [the Supreme Court of India] wanted to lock her up.

—*San Francisco Chronicle*

Writers have proved when they turn their back to power and start to feel the pulse and pain of society, they become powerful. This is the power beyond power that Arundhati Roy brings forth.

—Vandana Shiva

Powerful essays…that question everything from nuclear power, the so-called war against terror and the new imperialism.

—*Asian Week*

The fierceness with which Arundhati Roy loves humanity moves my heart. Her outrage at our needless suffering warms me. She is woman/artist/builder as we are, and can, and must be.

—Alice Walker

The scale of what Roy surveys is staggering. Her pointed indictment of India's hydroelectric industry—which has very little to show for the destruction it has wrought—is devastating.

—*New York Times Book Review*

With eloquent anger and careful research, Roy expertly captures the faces of both folly and courage.

—*Kirkus Reviews*

[Roy] is unequivocal in her criticism of U.S. foreign policy, but her zeal is illuminated by an abiding faith that there simply must be an alternative.

—*Village Voice*

If [Roy] continues to upset the globalization applecart like a Tom Paine pamphleteer, she will either be greatly honored or thrown in jail.

—*Wired Magazine*

The millions of readers who enjoyed *The God of Small Things* will find the same poetry and grace informing her [essays].

—Barnes & Noble.com

AN ORDINARY PERSON'S
GUIDE TO EMPIRE

ARUNDHATI ROY

South End Press
Cambridge, Massachusetts

Cover design by Elizabeth Elsas
Cover photo © by Martin Adler with permission from Panos Pictures
Text design and production by South End Press
First edition
Printed on recycled paper by union printers

Library of Congress Cataloging-in-Publication Data

Roy, Arundhati.
  An ordinary person's guide to empire / Arundhati Roy.
    p. cm.
  Includes bibliographical references and index.
  1. United States—Foreign relations—2001- 2. United States—Politics and government—2001- 3. Iraq War, 2003- 4. Imperialism. 5. World politics—1945-1989. 6. World politics—1989- 7. Globalization—Social aspects. 8. Globalization—Political aspects. 9. Social movements. 10. Mass media—Political aspects. I. Title.
E902.R696 2004
302.23'0973—dc22
                                    2004011169

South End Press, 7 Brookline Street, #1
Cambridge, MA 02139-4146
www.southendpress.org

09 08 07 06 05 04   1 2 3 4 5 6

Printed in Canada

CONTENTS

PEACE IS WAR

The Collateral Damage of Breaking News

There's been a delicious debate in the Indian press of late. A prominent English daily announced that it would sell space on page three (its gossip section) to anyone who was willing to pay to be featured. (The inference is that the rest of the news in the paper is in some way unsponsored, unsullied, "pure news.") The announcement provoked a series of responses—most of them outraged—that the proud tradition of impartial journalism could sink to such depths. Personally, I was delighted. For a major, mainstream newspaper to introduce the *notion* of "paid for" news is a giant step forward in the project of educating a largely credulous public about how the

This is the text of a speech first delivered March 7, 2003, at the Center for the Study of Developing Societies (CSDS), New Delhi, India, at a workshop organized by Sarai: The New Media Initiative, CSDS, and the Waag Society in Delhi. It was first published in the *Sarai Reader* 4: *Crisis/Media* (New Delhi: Sarai, 2004). See http://www.sarai.net/ for additional information on Sarai.

mass media operates. Once the idea of "paid for" news has been mooted, once it's been ushered through the portals of popular imagination, it won't be hard for people to work out that if gossip columns in newspapers can be auctioned, why not the rest of the column space? After all, in this age of the "market" when everything's up for sale—rivers, forests, freedom, democracy, and justice—what's special about news? Sponsored News—what a delectable idea! "This report is brought to you by…." There could be a state-regulated sliding scale for rates (headlines, page one, page two, sports section, and so on). Or on second thought we could leave that to be regulated by the "free market"—as it is now. Why change a winning formula?

The debate about whether mass-circulation newspapers and commercial TV channels are finely plotted ideological conspiracies or apolitical, benign anarchies that bumble along as best they can, is an old one and needs no elaboration. After the September 11 attack on the World Trade Center, the U.S. mainstream media's blatant performance as the government's mouthpiece was the butt of some pretty black humor in the rest of the world. It brought the myth of the Free Press in America crashing down. But before we gloat—the Indian mass media behaved no differently during the Pokhran nuclear tests and the Kargil War. There was no bumbling and very little was benign in the shameful coverage of the Decem-

Peace Is War

ber 13 attack on the Indian Parliament and the trial of S.A.R. Geelani, who has been sentenced to death after having been the subject of a media trial fueled by a campaign of nationalist hysteria and outright lies. On a more everyday basis: Would anybody who depends on the Indian mass media for information know that eighty thousand people have been killed in Kashmir since 1989, most of them Muslim, most of them by Indian security forces?[1] Most Indians would be outraged if it were suggested to them that the killings and "disappearances" in the Kashmir valley put India on a par with any banana republic.

Modern democracies have been around for long enough for neo-liberal capitalists to learn how to subvert them. They have mastered the technique of infiltrating the instruments of democracy—the "independent" judiciary, the "free" press, the parliament—and molding them to their purpose. The project of corporate globalization has cracked the code. Free elections, a free press, and an independent judiciary mean little when the free market has reduced them to commodities available on sale to the highest bidder.

To control a democracy, it is becoming more and more vital to control the media. The principal media outlets in America are owned by six major companies.[2] The six largest cable companies have eighty percent of cable television subscribers.[3] Even Internet websites are being colonized by giant media corporations.[4]

Arundhati Roy

It's a mistake to think that the corporate media supports the neo-liberal project. It *is* the neo-liberal project. It is the nexus, the confluence, the convergence, the union, the chosen medium of those who have power and money. As the project of corporate globalization increases the disparity between the rich and the poor, as the world grows more and more restive, corporations on the prowl for sweetheart deals need repressive governments to quell the mutinies in the servants' quarters. And governments, of course, need corporations. This mutual dependence spawns a sort of corporate nationalism, or, more accurately, a corporate/nationalism—if you can imagine such a thing. Corporate/nationalism has become the unwavering anthem of the mass media.

One of our main tasks is to expose the complex mess of cables that connect power to money to the supposedly "neutral" free press.

In the last couple of years, New Media has embarked on just such an enterprise. It has descended on Old Media like an annoying swarm of bees buzzing around an old buffalo, going where it goes, stopping where it stops, commenting on and critiquing its every move. New Media has managed not to transform, but to create the possibility of transforming conventional mass media from the sophisticated propaganda machine into a vast CD-ROM. Picture it: The old buffalo is the text, the bees are the hyperlinks that deconstruct it. Click a bee, get the inside story.

Basically, for the lucky few who have access to the Internet, the mass media has been contextualized and shown up for what it really is—an elaborate boardroom bulletin that reports and analyzes the concerns of powerful people. For the bees it's a phenomenal achievement. For the buffalo, obviously, it's not much fun.

For the bees (the nice, lefty ones) it's a significant victory, but by no means a conquest. Because it's still the annoyed buffalo stumbling across the plains, lurching from crisis to crisis, from war to war, who sets the pace. It's still the buffalo that decides which particular crisis will be the main course on the menu and what's for dessert. So here we are today, the buffalo and the bees—on the verge of a war that could redraw the political map of the world and alter the course of history. As the United States gears up to attack Iraq, the U.S. government's lies are being amplified, its reheated doctrine of pre-emptive strike talked up, its war machine deployed. There is still no sign of Iraq's so-called arsenal of weapons of mass destruction.

Even before the next phase of the war—the American occupation of Iraq—has begun (the war itself is thirteen years old), thanks to the busy bees the extent and scale, the speed and strength of the mobilization against the war has been unprecedented in history. On February 15, 2003, in an extraordinary display of public morality, millions of people took to the streets in hundreds of cities across the world, to protest against the invasion of Iraq.[5] If the U.S. government and its allies choose to ignore this and continue with their plans to invade and occupy Iraq, it could bring about a serious predicament in the modern world's understanding of democracy.

But then again, maybe we'll get used to it. Governments have learned to wait out crises—because they know that crises by definition must be short-lived. They know that a crisis-driven media simply cannot afford to hang about in the same place for too long. It must be off for its next appointment with the next crisis. Like business houses need a cash turnover, the media needs a crisis turnover. Whole countries become old news. They cease to exist. And the darkness becomes deeper than it was before the light was shone on them. We saw that in Afghanistan when the Soviets withdrew. We are being given a repeat performance now.

And eventually, when the buffalo stumbles away, the bees go, too.

Crisis reportage in the twenty-first century has evolved into an independent discipline—almost a science. The money, the technology, and the orchestrated mass hysteria that goes into crisis reporting has a curious effect. It isolates the crisis, unmoors it from the particularities of the history, the geography, and the culture that produced it. Eventually it floats free like a hot-air balloon, carrying its cargo of international gadflies—specialists, analysts, foreign correspondents, and crisis photographers with their enormous telephoto lenses.

Somewhere mid-journey and without prior notice, the gadflies auto-eject and parachute down to the site of the next crisis, leaving the crestfallen, abandoned balloon drifting aimlessly in the sky, pathetically masquerading as a current event, hoping it will at least make history.

There are few things sadder than a consumed, spent crisis. (For field research, look up Kabul, Afghanistan, 2002 A.D. and Gujarat, India, 2003 A.D.)

Crisis reportage has left us with a double-edged legacy. While governments hone the art of crisis management (the art of waiting out a crisis), resistance movements are increasingly being ensnared in a sort of vortex of crisis production. They have to find ways of precipitating crises, of manufacturing them in easily consumable, spectator-friendly formats. We have entered the era of crisis as a consumer item, crisis as spectacle, as theater. It's not new, but it's evolving, morphing, taking on new aspects. Flying planes into buildings is its most modern, most extreme form.

The disturbing thing nowadays is that Crisis as Spectacle has cut loose from its origins in genuine, long-term civil disobedience and is gradually becoming an instrument of resistance that is more symbolic than real. Also, it has begun to stray into other territory. Right now, it's blurring the lines that separate resistance movements from campaigns by political parties. I'm thinking here of L.K. Advani's Rath Yatra, which eventually led to the demolition of the Babri Masjid, and of the *"kar seva"* campaign for the construction of the Ram Temple at Ayodhya, which is brought to a boil by the Sangh Parivar each time elections come around.[6]

Both resistance movements and political election campaigns are in search of spectacle—though, of course, the kind of spectacle they choose differs vastly.

On the occasions when symbolic political theater shades into action that actually breaks the law, then it is the response of the State which usually provides the clarity to differentiate between a campaign by a political party and an action by a people's resistance movement. For instance, the police never opened fire on the rampaging mob that demolished the Babri Masjid, or those who participated in the genocidal campaign by the Congress Party against Sikhs in Delhi in 1984, or the Shiv Sena's massacre of Muslims in Bombay in 1993, or the Bajrang Dal's genocide against Muslims in Gujarat in 2002.[7] Neither the police, nor the courts, nor the government has taken serious action against anybody who participated in this violence.

Yet recently the police have repeatedly opened fire on unarmed people, including women and children, who have protested against the violation of their rights to life and livelihood by the government's "development projects."[8]

In this era of crisis reportage, if you don't have a crisis to call your own, you're not in the news. And if you're not in the news, you don't exist. It's as though the virtual world constructed in the media has become more real than the real world.

Every self-respecting people's movement, every "issue," needs to have its own hot-air balloon in the sky advertising its brand and purpose. For this reason, starvation deaths are more effective advertisements for drought and skewed food distribution, than cases of severe malnutrition—which don't quite make the cut. Standing in the rising water of a reservoir for days on end watching your home and belongings float away to protest against a big dam used to be an effective strategy, but isn't any more. People resisting dams are expected to either conjure new tricks or give up the struggle. In the despair created by the Indian Supreme Court's appalling judgment on the Sardar Sarovar Dam, senior activists of the Narmada Bachao Andolan (NBA) began once again to talk of *jal samarpan*—drowning themselves in the rising waters.[9] They were mocked for not really meaning what they said.

Crisis as a blood sport.

The Indian state and the mass media have shown themselves to be benignly tolerant of the phenomenon of Resistance as a Symbolic Spectacle. (It actually helps them to hold down the country's reputation as the world's biggest democracy). But whenever civil resistance has shown the slightest signs of metamorphosing from symbolic acts (dharnas, demonstrations, hunger strikes) into anything remotely resembling genuine civil disobedience—blockading villages, occupying forest land—the State has cracked down mercilessly.

In April 2001 the police opened fire on a peaceful meeting of the Adivasi Mukti Sangathan in Mehndi Kheda, Madhya Pradesh. On February 2, 2001, police fired on a peaceful protest of Munda Adivasis in Jharkhand, who were part of the protest against the Koel Karo hydroelectric, killing eight people and wounding twelve. On April 7, 2000, Gujarat police attacked a peaceful demonstration by the Kinara Bachao Sangharsh Samiti (the Save the Coast Action Committee) against the consortium of NATELCO and UNOCAL who were trying to do a survey for a proposed private port.[10] Lieutenant Colonel Pratap Save, one of the main activists, was beaten to death.[11] In Orissa, three Adivasis were killed for protesting a bauxite mining project in December 2000.[12] In Chilika, police fired on fisherfolk demanding the restoration of their fishing rights. Four people were killed.[13]

The instances of repression go on and on—Jambudweep, Kashipur, Maikanj. The most recent, of course, is the incident in the Muthanga in Wyanad, Kerala. In February 2003, four thousand displaced Adivasis, including women and children, occupied a small part of a wildlife sanctuary, demanding that they be given the land the government had promised them the previous year. The deadline had come and gone and there had been no sign that the government had any intention of keeping its word. As the tension built up over the days, the Kerala police surrounded the protestors and opened fire, killing one person and severely injuring several others.[14]

Interestingly, when it comes to the poor and, in particular, Dalit and Adivasi communities, they get killed for encroaching on forest land (Muthanga), as well as when they're trying to protect forest land from dams, mining operations, steel plants (Koel Karo, Nagarnar).[15]

In almost every instance of police firing, the State's strategy is to say the firing was provoked by an act of violence. Those who have been fired upon are immediately called militant (PWG, MCC, ISI, LTTE) agents.[16] In Muthanga, the police and the government claimed that the Adivasis had staged an armed insurrection and attempted to set up a parallel government. The speaker of the Kerala assembly said that they should have been "suppressed or shot."[17]

At the scene of the firing, the police had put together an "ammunition display." It consisted of some stones, a couple of sickles and axes, bows and arrows, and a few kitchen knives. One of the major weapons used in the uprising was a polythene bag full of bees.[18] (Imagine the young man collecting bees in the forest to protect himself and his little family against the Kerala police. What a delightful parallel government his would be!)

According to the State, when victims refuse to be victims, they become terrorists and are dealt with as such. They're either killed or arrested under POTA (Prevention of Terrorism Act). In states like Orissa, Bihar, and Jharkhand, which are rich in mineral resources and, therefore, vulnerable to ruthless corporations on the hunt, hundreds of villagers, including minors, have been arrested under POTA and are being held in jail without trial. Some states have special police battalions for "anti-development" activity. This is quite apart from the other use that POTA is being put to—terrorizing Muslims, particularly in states like Jammu and Kashmir and Gujarat. The space for genuine nonviolent civil disobedience is atrophying. In the era of corporate globalization, poverty is a crime, and protesting against further impoverishment is terrorism. In the era of the War on Terror, poverty is being slyly conflated with terrorism.

Calling anyone who protests against the violation of their human and constitutional rights a terrorist can end up becoming a self-fulfilling accusation. When every avenue of nonviolent dissent is closed down, should we really be surprised that the forests are filling up with extremists, insurgents, and militants? Vast parts of the country are already more or less beyond the control of the Indian state—Kashmir, the North East, large parts of Madhya Pradesh, Chhattisgarh, and Jharkhand.

It is utterly urgent for resistance movements and those of us who support them to reclaim the space for civil disobedience. To do this we will have to liberate ourselves from being manipulated, perverted, and headed off in the wrong direction by the desire to feed the media's endless appetite for theater. Because that saps energy and imagination.

There are signs that the battle has been joined. At a massive rally on February 27, 2003, the Nimad Malwa Kisan Mazdoor Sangathan (Nimad Malwa Farmers and Workers' Organization), in its protest against the privatization of power, declared that farmers and agricultural workers would not pay their electricity bills.[19] The Madhya Pradesh government has not yet responded. It'll be interesting to see what happens.

We have to find a way of forcing the real issues back into the news. For example, the real issue in the Narmada valley is not whether people will drown themselves or not. The NBA's strategies, its successes and failures are an issue, but a separate issue from the problem of big dams.

The real issue is that the privatization of essential infrastructure is essentially undemocratic. The real issue is the towering mass of incriminating evidence against big dams. The real issue is the fact that over the last fifty years in India alone big dams have displaced more than thirty-three million people.[20] The real issue is the fact that big dams are obsolete. They're ecologically destructive, economically unviable, and politically undemocratic. The real issue is the fact that the Supreme Court of India ordered the construction of the Sardar Sarovar Dam to proceed even though it is aware that it violates the fundamental rights to life and livelihood of the citizens of India.[21]

Unfortunately, the mass media, through a combination of ignorance and design, has framed the whole argument as one between those who are pro-development and those who are anti-development. It slyly suggests that the NBA is anti-electricity and anti-irrigation. And, of course, anti-Gujarat. This is complete nonsense. The NBA believes that big dams are obsolete. They're not just bad for displaced people, they're bad for Gujarat, too. They're too expensive, the water will not go where it's supposed to, and eventually the area that is supposed to "benefit" will pay a heavy price. Like what is happening in the command area of India's favorite dam—the Bhakra Nangal.[22] The NBA believes that there are more local, more democratic, ecologically sustainable, economically viable ways of generating electricity and managing water systems. It is demanding more modernity, not less. More democracy, not less.

Peace Is War

After the Supreme Court delivered what is generally considered to be a knockout blow to the most spectacular resistance movement in India, the vultures are back, circling over the kill. The World Bank's new *Water Resources Sector Strategy* clarifies that the World Bank will return to its policy of funding big dams.[23] Meanwhile the Indian government, directed by the venerable Supreme Court, has trundled out an ancient, hairbrained, Stalinist scheme of linking India's rivers. The order was given based on no real information or research—just on the whim of an aging judge.[24] The river-linking project makes big dams look like enlightenment itself. It will become to the development debate what the Ram Mandir in Ayodhya is to the communal debate—a venal campaign gimmick that can be rolled out just before every election. It is destructive even if it is never realized. It will be used to block every other more local, more effective, more democratic irrigation project. It will be used to siphon off enormous sums of public money.

Linking India's rivers would lead to massive social upheavals and ecological devastation. Any modern ecologist who hears about this plan bursts out laughing. Yet leading papers and journals like *India Today* and *Indian Express* carry laudatory pieces full of absurd information.

Coming back to the tyranny of crisis reportage: One way to cut loose is to understand that for most people in the world, peace is war—a daily battle against hunger, thirst, and the violation of their dignity. Wars are often the end result of a flawed peace, a putative peace. And it is the flaws, the systemic flaws in what is normally *considered* to be "peace," that we ought to be writing about. We have to—at least some of us have to—become peace correspondents instead of war correspondents. We have to lose our terror of the mundane. We have to use our skills and imagination and our art, to re-create the rhythms of the endless crisis of normality, and in doing so, expose the policies and processes that make ordinary things—food, water, shelter, and dignity—such a distant dream for ordinary people.

Most important of all, we have to turn our skills toward understanding and exposing the instruments of the State. In India, for instance, the institution that is least scrutinized and least accountable takes every major political, cultural, and executive decision today. The Indian Supreme Court is one of the most powerful courts in the world. It decides whether dams should be built or not, whether slums should be cleared, whether industry should be removed from urban areas. It takes decisions on issues like privatization and disinvestment. On the content of school textbooks. It micro-manages our lives. Its orders affect the lives of millions of people. Whether you agree with the Supreme Court's decisions—all of them, some of them, none of them—or not, as an institution the Supreme Court has to be accountable. In a democracy, you have checks and balances, not hierarchies. And yet, because of the

Peace Is War

Contempt of Court law, we cannot criticize the Supreme Court or call it to account. How can you have an undemocratic institution in a democratic society? It will automatically become a floor trap that accumulates authority, that confers supreme powers on itself. And that's exactly what has happened. We live in a judicial dictatorship. And we don't seem to have even begun to realize it.

The only way to make democracy real is to begin a process of constant questioning, permanent provocation, and continuous public conversation between citizens and the State. That conversation is quite different from the conversation between political parties. (Representing the views of rival political parties is what the mass media thinks of as "balanced" reporting.) Patrolling the borders of our liberty is the only way we can guard against the snatching away of our freedoms. All over the world today, freedoms are being curbed in the name of protecting freedom. Once freedoms are surrendered by civil society, they cannot be retrieved without a struggle. It is so much easier to relinquish them than to recover them.

It is important to remember that our freedoms, such as they are, were never given to us by any government, they have been wrested by us. If we do not use them, if we do not test them from time to time, they atrophy. If we do not guard them constantly, they will be taken away from us. If we do not demand more and more, we will be left with less and less.

Understanding these things and then using them as tools to interrogate what we consider "normalcy" is a way of subverting the tyranny of crisis reportage.

Finally, there's another worrying kind of collateral damage caused by crisis reportage. Crisis reportage flips history over, turns it belly-up. It tells stories back to front. So we begin with the news of a crisis, and end (if we're lucky) with an account of the events that led to it. For example, we enter the history of Afghanistan through the debris of the World Trade Center in New York, the history of Iraq through Operation Desert Storm. We enter the story of the Adivasi struggle for justice in Kerala through the news of police firing on those who dared to encroach on a wildlife sanctuary. So crisis reportage forces us to view a complex evolving historical process through the distorting prism of a single current event.

Crises polarize people. They hustle us into making uninformed choices: "You're either with us or with the terrorists." "You're either pro-privatization or pro-State." "If you're not pro-Bush, you're pro-Saddam Hussein." "If you're not good, you're evil."

These are spurious choices. They're not the only ones available to us. But in a crisis, we become like goal-keepers in a penalty shoot-out of a soccer match. We imagine that we have to commit ourselves to one side or another. We have nothing to go on but instinct and social conditioning. And once we're committed, it's hard to realign oneself. In this process, those who ought to be natural allies become enemies.

For example, when the police fired on the Adivasis who "encroached" on the wildlife sanctuary in Muthanga, Kerala, environmentalists did not come to their defense because they were outraged that the Adivasis had dared to encroach on a wildlife sanctuary. In actual fact the "sanctuary" was a eucalyptus plantation.[25] Years ago, old-growth forest had been clear-felled by the government to plant eucalyptus for the Birla's Grasim Rayon Factory, set up in 1958. A huge mass of incriminating data accuses the factory of devastating the bamboo forests in the region, polluting the Chaliyar River, emitting toxins into the air, and causing a great deal of suffering to a great number of people.[26] In the name of employing three thousand people, it destroyed the livelihood of what has been estimated to be about three hundred thousand bamboo workers, sand miners, and fisherfolk. The state government did nothing to control the pollution or the destruction of forests and rivers. There were no police firing at the owners or managers of Grasim. But then, they had not committed the crime of being poor, being Adivasi, or being on the brink of starvation. When the natural resources (bamboo, eucalyptus, pulp) ran out, the factory closed down. The workers were abandoned.[27]

Crisis reportage elides these facts and forces people to make uninformed choices.

The real crisis—the dispossession, the disempowerment, the daily violation of the democratic rights and the dignity of not thousands but millions of people, which has been set into motion not by accident but by deliberate design—does not fit into the predetermined format of crisis reporting.

Fifteen years ago, the corrupt, centralized Indian state was too grand, too top-heavy, and too far away for its poor to have access to it—to its institutions of education, of health, of water supply, and of electricity. Even its sewage system was inaccessible, too good for most. Today, the project of corporate globalization has increased the distance between those who take the decisions and those who must suffer them even more. For the poor, the uneducated, the displaced and dispossessed, that distance puts justice out of reach.

So the unrelenting daily grind of injustice goes unreported and the silent, unformatted battle spreads subcutaneously through our society, ushering us toward a future that doesn't bear thinking about.

But we continue sailing on our *Titanic* as it tilts slowly into the darkened sea. The deckhands panic. Those with cheaper tickets have begun to be washed away. But in the banquet halls, the music plays on. The only signs of trouble are slightly slanting waiters, the kabobs and canapés sliding to one side of their silver trays, the somewhat exaggerated sloshing of the wine in the crystal wineglasses. The rich are comforted by the knowledge that the lifeboats on the deck are reserved for club-class passengers. The tragedy is that they are probably right.

THE ORDINARY PERSON'S GUIDE TO EMPIRE

Mesopotamia. Babylon. The Tigris and Euphrates. How many children in how many classrooms, over how many centuries, have hang-glided through the past, transported on the wings of these words?

And now the bombs are falling, incinerating, and humiliating that ancient civilization.

On the steel torsos of their missiles, adolescent American soldiers scrawl colorful messages in childish handwriting: "For Saddam, from the Fat Boy Posse."[1] A building goes down. A marketplace. A home. A girl who loves a boy. A child who only ever wanted to play with his older brother's marbles.

On March 21, the day after American and British troops began their illegal invasion and occupation of Iraq, an "embedded" CNN correspondent interviewed an American sol-

---

The original version of this essay was first published in *The Guardian* (London), April 2, 2003.

dier. "I wanna get in there and get my nose dirty," Private AJ said. "I wanna take revenge for 9/11."[2]

To be fair to the correspondent, even though he was "embedded," he did sort of weakly suggest that so far there was no real evidence that linked the Iraqi government to the September 11 attacks. Private AJ stuck his teenage tongue out all the way down to the end of his chin. "Yeah, well, that stuff's way over my head," he said.[3]

According to a *New York Times*/CBS News survey, forty-two percent of the American public believes that Saddam Hussein is directly responsible for the September 11 attacks on the World Trade Center and the Pentagon.[4] And an ABC News poll says that fifty-five percent of Americans believe that Saddam Hussein directly supports Al-Qaeda.[5] What percentage of America's armed forces believes these fabrications is anybody's guess.

It is unlikely that British and American troops fighting in Iraq are aware that their governments supported Saddam Hussein both politically and financially through his worst excesses.

But why should poor AJ and his fellow soldiers be burdened with these details? It doesn't matter any more, does it? Hundreds of thousands of men, tanks, ships, choppers, bombs, ammunition, gas masks, high-protein food, whole aircrafts ferrying toilet paper, insect repellent, vitamins, and bottled mineral water are on the move. The phenomenal logistics of Operation Iraqi Freedom make it a universe unto itself. It doesn't need to justify its existence any more. It exists. It *is*.

President George W. Bush, commander in chief of the U.S. Army, Navy, Air Force, and Marines, has issued clear instructions: "Iraq. Will. Be. Liberated."[6] (Perhaps he means that even if Iraqi people's bodies are killed, their souls will be liberated.) American and British citizens owe it to the Supreme Commander to forsake thought and rally behind their troops. Their countries are at war.

And what a war it is.

After using the "good offices" of U.N. diplomacy (economic sanctions and weapons inspections) to ensure that Iraq was brought to its knees, its people starved, half a million of its children killed, its infrastructure severely damaged, after making sure that most of its weapons have been destroyed, in an act of cowardice that must surely be unrivaled in history, the "Allies"/"Coalition of the Willing" (better known as the Coalition of the Bullied and Bought) sent in an invading army!

Operation Iraqi Freedom? I don't think so. It's more like Operation Let's Run a Race, but First Let Me Break Your Knees.

So far the Iraqi army, with its hungry, ill-equipped soldiers, its old guns and aging tanks, has somehow managed to temporarily confound and occasionally even out-maneuver the "Allies." Faced with the richest, best-equipped, most powerful armed forces the world has ever seen, Iraq has shown spectacular courage and has even managed to put up what actually amounts to a defense. A defense which the Bush/Blair Pair have immediately denounced as deceitful and cowardly. (But then deceit is an old tradition with us natives. When we're invaded/colonized/occupied and stripped of all dignity, we turn to guile and opportunism.)

Even allowing for the fact that Iraq and the "Allies" are at war, the extent to which the "Allies" and their media cohorts are prepared to go is astounding to the point of being counterproductive to their own objectives.

When Saddam Hussein appeared on national TV to address the Iraqi people following the failure of the most elaborate assassination attempt in history—Operation Decapitation—we had Geoff Hoon, British defense secretary, deriding him for not having the courage to stand up and be killed, calling him a coward who hides in trenches.[7] We then had a flurry of coalition speculation—Was it really Saddam Hussein, was it his double? Or was it Osama with a shave? Was it pre-recorded? Was it a speech? Was it black magic? Will it turn into a pumpkin if we really, really want it to?

After dropping not hundreds, but thousands, of bombs on Baghdad, when a marketplace was mistakenly blown up and civilians killed, a U.S. army spokesman implied that the

The Ordinary Person's Guide to Empire

Iraqis were blowing themselves up! "They're also using very old stocks…and those stocks are not reliable, and [their] missiles are going up and coming down."[8]

If so, may we ask how this squares with the accusation that the Iraqi regime is a paid-up member of the Axis of Evil and a threat to world peace?

When the Arab TV station Al-Jazeera shows civilian casualties, it's denounced as "emotive" Arab propaganda aimed at orchestrating hostility toward the "Allies," as though Iraqis are dying only in order to make the "Allies" look bad. Even French television has come in for some stick for similar reasons. But the awed, breathless footage of aircraft carriers, stealth bombers, and cruise missiles arcing across the desert sky on American and British TV is described as the "terrible beauty" of war.[9]

When invading American soldiers (from the army "that's only here to help") are taken prisoner and shown on Iraqi TV, George Bush says it violates the Geneva Convention and exposes "the Iraqi regime and the evil at its heart."[10] But it is entirely acceptable for U.S. television stations to show the hundreds of prisoners being held by the U.S. government in Guantánamo Bay, kneeling on the ground with their hands tied behind their backs, blinded with opaque goggles and with earphones clamped on their ears, to ensure complete visual and aural deprivation.[11] When questioned about the treatment of prisoners in Guantánamo Bay, U.S. government officials don't deny that they're being ill-treated. They deny that they're prisoners of war! They call them "unlawful combatants,"[12] implying that their ill-treatment is legitimate! (So what's the party line on the massacre of prisoners in Mazar-e-Sharif, Afghanistan?[13] Forgive and forget? And what of the prisoner tortured to death by the Special Forces at the Bagram Air Force Base? Doctors have formally called it homicide.[14])

When the "Allies" bombed the Iraqi television station (also, incidentally, a contravention of the Geneva Convention), there was vulgar jubilation in the American media. In fact, Fox TV had been lobbying for the attack for a while.[15] It was seen as a righteous blow against Arab propaganda. But mainstream American and British TV continue to advertise themselves as "balanced" when their propaganda has achieved hallucinatory levels.

Why should propaganda be the exclusive preserve of the Western media? Just because they do it better?

Western journalists "embedded" with troops are given the status of heroes reporting from the front lines of war. Non-"embedded" journalists (like the BBC's Rageh Omaar, reporting from besieged and bombed Baghdad, witnessing, and clearly affected by, the sight of bodies of burned children and wounded people[16]) are undermined even before they be-

gin their reportage: "We have to tell you that he is being moni-
tored by the Iraqi Authorities."

Increasingly, on British and American TV, Iraqi soldiers
are being referred to as "militia" (i.e., rabble). One BBC correspondent portentously referred to them as "quasi-terrorists."
Iraqi defense is "resistance" or, worse still, "pockets of resistance," Iraqi military strategy is deceit. (The U.S. government
bugging the phone lines of U.N. Security Council delegates,
reported by the London *Observer*, is hardheaded pragmatism.[17])
Clearly for the "Allies" the only morally acceptable strategy the
Iraqi army can pursue is to march out into the desert and be
bombed by B-52s or be mowed down by machine-gun fire.
Anything short of that is cheating.

And now we have the siege of Basra. About a million and
a half people, forty percent of them children.[18] Without clean
water, and with very little food. We're still waiting for the leg-
endary Shia "uprising," for the happy hordes to stream out of
the city and rain roses and hosannahs on the "liberating" army.
Where are the hordes? Don't they know that television pro-
ductions work to tight schedules? (It may well be that if the
Saddam Hussein regime falls there will be dancing on the
streets the world over.)

After days of enforcing hunger and thirst on the citizens
of Basra, the "Allies" have brought in a few trucks of food and
water and positioned them tantalizingly on the outskirts of the

city. Desperate people flock to the trucks and fight each other for food. (The water, we hear, is being sold.[19] To revitalize the dying economy, you understand.) On top of the trucks, desperate photographers fought each other to get pictures of desperate people fighting each other for food. Those pictures will go out through photo agencies to newspapers and glossy magazines that pay extremely well. Their message: The messiahs are at hand, distributing fishes and loaves.

As of July 2002, the delivery of $5.4 billion worth of supplies to Iraq was blocked by the Bush/Blair Pair.[20] It didn't really make the news. But now, under the loving caress of live TV, two hundred and thirty tons of humanitarian aid—a minuscule fraction of what's actually needed (call it a script prop)—arrived on a British ship, the *Sir Galahad*.[21] Its arrival in the port of Umm Qasr merited a whole day of live TV broadcasts. Barf bag, anyone?

Nick Guttmann, head of emergencies for Christian Aid, writing for the *Independent on Sunday*, said that it would take thirty-two *Sir Galahad*s a day to match the amount of food Iraq was receiving before the bombing began.[22]

We oughtn't to be surprised, though. It's old tactics. They've been at it for years. Remember this moderate proposal by John McNaughton from the *Pentagon Papers* published during the Vietnam War.

The Ordinary Person's Guide to Empire

Strikes at population targets (per se) are likely not only to create a counterproductive wave of revulsion abroad and at home, but greatly to increase the risk of enlarging the war with China or the Soviet Union. Destruction of locks and dams, however—if handled right—might…offer promise. Such destruction does not kill or drown people. By shallow-flooding the rice, it leads after time to widespread starvation (more than a million?) unless food is provided—which we could offer to do "at the conference table."[23]

Times haven't changed very much. The technique has evolved into a doctrine. It's called "Winning Hearts and Minds."

So, here's the moral math as it stands: Two hundred thousand Iraqis estimated to have been killed in the first Gulf War.[24] Hundreds of thousands dead because of the economic sanctions. (At least that lot has been saved from Saddam Hussein.) More being killed every day. Tens of thousands of U.S. soldiers who fought the 1991 war officially declared "disabled" by a disease called Gulf War Syndrome believed in part to be caused by exposure to depleted uranium.[25] It hasn't stopped the "Allies" from continuing to use depleted uranium.[26]

31

And now this talk of bringing the United Nations back into the picture.

But that old U.N. girl—it turns out that she just ain't what she was cracked up to be. She's been demoted (although she retains her high salary). Now she's the world's janitor. She's the Filipina cleaning lady, the Indian jamadarni, the mail-order bride from Thailand, the Mexican household help, the Jamaican au pair. She's employed to clean other people's shit. She's used and abused at will.

Despite Tony Blair's earnest submissions, and all his fawning, George Bush has made it clear that the United Nations will play no independent part in the administration of post-war Iraq. The United States will decide who gets those juicy "reconstruction" contracts.[27] But Bush has appealed to the international community not to "politicize" the issue of humanitarian aid. On March 28, 2003, after Bush called for the immediate resumption of the U.N.'s Oil for Food program, the U.N. Security Council voted unanimously for the resolution.[28] This means that everybody agrees that Iraqi money (from the sale of Iraqi oil) should be used to feed Iraqi people who are starving because of U.S.-led sanctions and the illegal U.S.-led war.

Contracts for the "reconstruction" of Iraq, we're told, in discussions on the business news, could jump-start the world economy. It's funny how the interests of American corporations are so often, so successfully, and so deliberately confused with the interests of the world economy. While the American people will end up paying for the war, oil companies, weapons manufacturers, arms dealers, and corporations involved in "reconstruction" work will make direct gains from the war. Many of them are old friends and former employers of the Bush/Cheney/Rumsfeld/Rice cabal. Bush has already asked Congress for seventy-five billion dollars.[29] Contracts for "reconstruction" are already being negotiated. The news doesn't hit the stands because much of the U.S. corporate media is owned and managed by the same interests.

Operation Iraqi Freedom, Tony Blair assures us, is about returning Iraqi oil to the Iraqi people. That is, returning Iraqi oil to the Iraqi people via corporate multinationals. Like Shell, like Chevron, like Halliburton. Or are we missing the plot here? Perhaps Halliburton is actually an Iraqi company? Perhaps U.S. Vice President Dick Cheney (who was a former director of Halliburton) is a closet Iraqi?

As the rift between Europe and America deepens, there are signs that the world could be entering a new era of economic boycotts. CNN reported that Americans are emptying French wine into gutters, chanting "We don't need your stinking wine."[30] We've heard about the re-baptism of french fries. Freedom fries, they're called now.[31] There's news trickling in about Americans boycotting German goods.[32] The thing is that if the fallout of the war takes this turn, it is the United States who will suffer the most. Its homeland may be defended by border patrols and nuclear weapons, but its economy is strung out across the globe. Its economic outposts are exposed and vulnerable to attack in every direction. Already the Internet is buzzing with elaborate lists of American and British government products and companies that should be boycotted. These lists are being honed and refined by activists across the world. They could become a practical guide that directs and channels the amorphous but growing fury in the world. Suddenly, the "inevitability" of the project of corporate globalization is beginning to seem more than a little evitable.

It's become clear that the War against Terror is not really about terror, and the War on Iraq not only about oil. It's about a superpower's self-destructive impulse toward supremacy, stranglehold, global hegemony. The argument is being made that the people of Argentina and Iraq have both been decimated by the same process. Only the weapons used against them differ: In the one case it's an IMF checkbook. In the other, the cruise missiles.

Finally, there's the matter of Saddam Hussein's arsenal of Weapons of Mass Destruction. (Oops, nearly forgot about those!)

In the fog of war one thing's for sure: If the Saddam Hussein regime indeed has weapons of mass destruction, it is showing an astonishing degree of responsibility and restraint in the teeth of extreme provocation. Under similar circumstances (say, if Iraqi troops were bombing New York and laying siege to Washington, D.C.) could we expect the same of the Bush regime? Would it keep its thousands of nuclear warheads in their wrapping paper? What about its chemical and biological weapons? Its stocks of anthrax, smallpox, and nerve gas? Would it?

Excuse me while I laugh.

In the fog of war we're forced to speculate: Either Saddam Hussein is an extremely responsible tyrant. Or—he simply does not possess Weapons of Mass Destruction. Either way, regardless of what happens next, Iraq comes out of the argument smelling sweeter than the U.S. government.

So here's Iraq—rogue state, grave threat to world peace, paid-up member of the Axis of Evil. Here's Iraq, invaded, bombed, besieged, bullied, its sovereignty shat upon, its children killed by cancers, its people blown up on the streets. And here's all of us watching CNN–BBC, BBC–CNN late into the night. Here's all of us, enduring the horror of the war, enduring the horror of the propaganda, and enduring the slaughter of language as we know and understand it. Freedom now means mass murder (or, in the United States, fried potatoes). When someone says "humanitarian aid" we automatically go looking for induced starvation. "Embedded," I have to admit, is a great find. It's what it sounds like. And what about "arsenal of tactics"? Nice!

In most parts of the world, the invasion of Iraq is being seen as a racist war. The real danger of a racist war unleashed by racist regimes is that it engenders racism in every-body—perpetrators, victims, spectators. It sets the parameters for the debate, it lays out a grid for a particular way of thinking. There is a tidal wave of hatred for the United States rising from the ancient heart of the world. In Africa, Latin America, Asia, Europe, Australia. I encounter it every day. Sometimes it comes from the most unlikely sources. Bankers, businessmen, yuppie students, who bring to it all the crassness of their conservative, illiberal politics. That absurd inability to separate governments from people: America is a nation of morons, a nation of mur-derers, they say (with the same carelessness with which they say, "All Muslims are terrorists"). Even in the grotesque universe of racist insult, the British make their entry as add-ons. Arse-lickers, they're called.

Suddenly, I, who have been vilified for being "anti-American" and "anti-West," find myself in the extraordi-nary position of defending the people of America. And Britain.

Those who descend so easily into the pit of racist abuse would do well to remember the hundreds of thousands of American and British citizens who protested against their country's stockpile of nuclear weapons. And the thousands of

American war resisters who forced their government to withdraw from Vietnam. They should know that the most scholarly, scathing, hilarious critiques of the U.S. government and the "American Way of Life" come from American citizens. And that the funniest, most bitter condemnation of their prime minister comes from the British media. Finally, they should remember that right now, hundreds of thousands of British and American citizens are on the streets protesting the war. The Coalition of the Bullied and Bought consists of governments, not people. More than a third of America's citizens have survived the relentless propaganda they've been subjected to, and many thousands are actively fighting their own government. In the ultra-patriotic climate that prevails in the United States, that's as brave as any Iraqi fighting for his or her homeland.

While the "Allies" wait in the desert for an uprising of Shia Muslims on the streets of Basra, the real uprising is taking place in hundreds of cities across the world. It has been the most spectacular display of public morality ever seen.

Most courageous of all are the hundreds of thousands of American people on the streets of America's great cities—Washington, New York, Chicago, San Francisco. The fact is that the only institution in the world today that is more powerful than the American government is American civil society. American citizens have a huge responsibility riding on their shoulders. How can we not salute and support those who not only acknowledge but act upon that responsibility? They are our allies, our friends.

At the end of it all, it remains to be said that dictators like Saddam Hussein, and all the other despots in the Middle East, in the Central Asian republics, in Africa, and Latin America, many of them installed, supported, and financed by the U.S. government, are a menace to their own people. Other than strengthening the hand of civil society (instead of weakening it as has been done in the case of Iraq), there is no easy, pristine way of dealing with them. (It's odd how those who dismiss the peace movement as utopian don't hesitate to proffer the most absurdly dreamy reasons for going to war: To stamp out terrorism, install democracy, eliminate fascism, and, most entertainingly, to "rid the world of evil-doers."[33])

Regardless of what the propaganda machine tells us, these tin-pot dictators are not the greatest threat to the world. The real and pressing danger, the greatest threat of all, is the locomotive force that drives the political and economic engine of the U.S. government, currently piloted by George Bush. Bush-bashing is fun, because he makes such an easy, sumptuous target. It's true that he is a dangerous, almost suicidal pilot, but the machine he handles is far more dangerous than the man himself.

The Ordinary Person's Guide to Empire

Despite the pall of gloom that hangs over us today, I'd like to file a cautious plea for hope: In time of war, one wants one's weakest enemy at the helm of his forces. And President George W. Bush is certainly that. Any other even averagely intelligent U.S. president would have probably done the very same things, but would have managed to smoke up the glass and confuse the opposition. Perhaps even carry the United Nations with him. George Bush's tactless imprudence and his brazen belief that he can run the world with his riot squad has done the opposite. He has achieved what writers, activists, and scholars have striven to achieve for decades. He has exposed the ducts. He has placed on full public view the working parts, the nuts and bolts of the apocalyptic apparatus of the American Empire.

Now that the blueprint, The Ordinary Person's Guide to Empire, has been put into mass circulation, it could be disabled quicker than the pundits predicted.

Bring on the spanners.

INSTANT-MIX IMPERIAL DEMOCRACY

(Buy One, Get One Free)

In these times when we have to race to keep abreast of the speed at which our freedoms are being snatched from us, and when few can afford the luxury of retreating from the streets for a while in order to return with an exquisite, fully formed political thesis replete with footnotes and references, what profound gift can I offer you tonight?

As we lurch from crisis to crisis, beamed directly into our brains by satellite TV, we have to think on our feet. On the move. We enter histories through the rubble of war. Ruined cities, parched fields, shrinking forests and dying rivers are our archives. Craters left by daisy cutters, our libraries.

This talk was first delivered May 13, 2003, at the Riverside Church, New York City, and broadcast live on Pacifica Radio. The lecture, sponsored by the Lannan Foundation and the Center for Economic and Social Rights, was delivered as an acceptance speech for the 2002 Lannan Prize for Cultural Freedom.

41

So what can I offer you tonight? Some uncomfortable thoughts about money, war, empire, racism, and democracy. Some worries that flit around my brain like a family of persistent moths that keep me awake at night.

Some of you will think it bad manners for a person like me, officially entered in the Big Book of Modern Nations as an "Indian citizen," to come here and criticize the U.S. government. Speaking for myself, I'm no flag-waver, no patriot, and am fully aware that venality, brutality, and hypocrisy are imprinted on the leaden soul of every state. But when a country ceases to be merely a country and becomes an empire, then the scale of operations changes dramatically. So may I clarify that tonight I speak as a subject of the American empire? I speak as a slave who presumes to criticize her king.

Since lectures must be called something, mine tonight is called Instant-Mix Imperial Democracy (Buy One, Get One Free).

Way back in 1988, on July 3, the U.S.S. *Vincennes,* a missile cruiser stationed in the Persian Gulf, accidentally shot down an Iranian airliner and killed two hundred and ninety civilian passengers.[1] George Bush the First, who was at the time on his presidential campaign, was asked to comment on the incident. He said quite subtly, "I will never apologize for the United States. I don't care what the facts are."[2]

Instant-Mix Imperial Democracy

I don't care what the facts are. What a perfect maxim for the New American Empire. Perhaps a slight variation on the theme would be more apposite: The facts can be whatever we want them to be.

When the United States invaded Iraq, a *New York Times*/CBS News survey estimated that forty-two percent of the American public believed that Saddam Hussein was directly responsible for the September 11 attacks on the World Trade Center and the Pentagon.[3] And an ABC News poll said that fifty-five percent of Americans believed that Saddam Hussein directly supported Al-Qaeda.[4] None of this opinion is based on evidence (because there isn't any). All of it is based on insinuation, auto-suggestion, and outright lies circulated by the U.S. corporate media, otherwise known as the "Free Press," that hollow pillar on which contemporary American democracy rests.

Public support in the United States for the war against Iraq was founded on a multi-tiered edifice of falsehood and deceit, coordinated by the U.S. government and faithfully amplified by the corporate media.

Apart from the invented links between Iraq and Al-Qaeda, we had the manufactured frenzy about Iraq's Weapons of Mass Destruction. George Bush the Lesser went to the extent of saying it would be "suicide" for the United States not to attack Iraq.[5] We once again witnessed the para-

noia that a starved, bombed, besieged country was about to
annihilate almighty America. (Iraq was only the latest in a suc-
cession of countries—earlier there was Cuba, Nicaragua,
Libya, Grenada, Panama). But this time it wasn't just your ordinary brand of friendly neighborhood frenzy. It was frenzy
with a purpose. It ushered in an old doctrine in a new bottle:
the doctrine of pre-emptive strike, a.k.a. The United States
Can Do Whatever The Hell It Wants, And That's Official.

The war against Iraq has been fought and won and no
Weapons of Mass Destruction have been found. Not even a
little one. Perhaps they'll have to be planted before they're dis-
covered. And then the more troublesome amongst us will
need an explanation for why Saddam Hussein didn't use them
when his country was being invaded.

Of course, there'll be no answers. True believers will make
do with those fuzzy TV reports about the discovery of a few
barrels of banned chemicals in an old shed. There seems to be
no consensus yet about whether they're really chemicals,
whether they're actually banned, and whether the vessels
they're contained in can technically be called barrels. (There
were unconfirmed rumors that a teaspoonful of potassium
permanganate and an old harmonica were found there, too.)

Meanwhile, in passing, an ancient civilization has been casually decimated by a very recent, casually brutal nation.

Instant-Mix Imperial Democracy

Then there are those who say, so what if Iraq had no chemical and nuclear weapons? So what if there is no Al-Qaeda connection? So what if Osama bin Laden hates Saddam Hussein as much as he hates the United States? Bush the Lesser has said Saddam Hussein was a "Homicidal Dictator."[6] And so, the reasoning goes, Iraq needed a "regime change."

Never mind that forty years ago, the CIA, under President John F. Kennedy, orchestrated a regime change in Baghdad. In 1963, after a successful coup, the Ba'ath party came to power in Iraq. Using lists provided by the CIA, the new Ba'ath regime systematically eliminated hundreds of doctors, teachers, lawyers, and political figures known to be leftists.[7] An entire intellectual community was slaughtered. (The same technique was used to massacre hundreds of thousands of people in Indonesia and East Timor.[8]) The young Saddam Hussein was said to have had a hand in supervising the bloodbath. In 1979, after factional infighting within the Ba'ath Party, Saddam Hussein became the president of Iraq. In April 1980, while Hussein was massacring Shias, U.S. National Security Adviser Zbigniew Brzezinski declared, "We see no fundamental incompatibility of interests between the United States and Iraq."[9] Washington and London overtly and covertly supported Saddam Hussein. They financed him, equipped him, armed him, and provided him with dual-use materials to man-

45

ufacture weapons of mass destruction.[10] They supported his worst excesses financially, materially, and morally. They supported the eight-year war against Iran and the 1988 gassing of Kurdish people in Halabja, crimes which fourteen years later were reheated and served up as reasons to justify invading Iraq.[11] After the first Gulf War, the "Allies" fomented an uprising of Shias in Basra and then looked away while Saddam Hussein crushed the revolt and slaughtered thousands in an act of vengeful reprisal.[12]

The point is, if Saddam Hussein was evil enough to merit the most elaborate, openly declared assassination attempt in history (the opening move of Operation Shock and Awe), then surely those who supported him ought at least to be tried for war crimes? Why aren't the faces of U.S. and U.K. government officials on the infamous pack of cards of wanted men and women?

Because when it comes to Empire, facts don't matter.

Yes, but all that's in the past, we're told. Saddam Hussein is a monster who must be stopped now. And only the United States can stop him. It's an effective technique, this use of the urgent morality of the present to obscure the diabolical sins of the past and the malevolent plans for the future. Indonesia, Panama, Nicaragua, Iraq, Afghanistan—the list goes on and on. Right now there are brutal regimes being groomed for the

Instant-Mix Imperial Democracy

future—Egypt, Saudi Arabia, Turkey, Pakistan, the Central Asian republics.

U.S. Attorney General John Ashcroft recently declared that U.S. freedoms are "not the grant of any government or document, but ... our endowment from God."[13] (Why bother with the United Nations when God himself is on hand?)

So here we are, the people of the world, confronted with an Empire armed with a mandate from heaven (and, as added insurance, the most formidable arsenal of weapons of mass destruction in history). Here we are, confronted with an Empire that has conferred upon itself the right to go to war at will and the right to deliver people from corrupting ideologies, from religious fundamentalists, dictators, sexism, and poverty, by the age-old, tried-and-tested practice of extermination. Empire is on the move, and Democracy is its sly new war cry. Democracy, home-delivered to your doorstep by daisy-cutters. Death is a small price for people to pay for the privilege of sampling this new product: Instant-Mix Imperial Democracy (bring to a boil, add oil, then bomb).

But then perhaps chinks, negroes, dinks, gooks, and wogs don't really qualify as real people. Perhaps our deaths don't qualify as real deaths. Our histories don't qualify as history. They never have.

Speaking of history, in these past months, while the world watched, the U.S. invasion and occupation of Iraq was broadcast on live TV. Like Osama bin Laden and the Taliban in Afghanistan, the regime of Saddam Hussein simply disappeared. This was followed by what analysts called a "power vacuum."[14] Cities that had been under siege, without food, water, and electricity for days, cities that had been bombed relentlessly, people who had been starved and systematically impoverished by the U.N. sanctions regime for more than a decade, were suddenly left with no semblance of urban administration. A seven-thousand-year-old civilization slid into anarchy. On live TV.

Vandals plundered shops, offices, hotels, and hospitals. American and British soldiers stood by and watched.[15] They said they had no orders to act. In effect, they had orders to kill people, but not to protect them. Their priorities were clear. The safety and security of Iraqi people was not their business. The security of whatever little remained of Iraq's infrastructure was not their business. But the security and safety of Iraq's oil fields were. Of course they were. The oil fields were "secured" almost before the invasion began.[16]

On CNN and the BBC the scenes of the rampage were played and replayed. TV commentators, army and government spokespersons portrayed it as a "liberated people" venting their rage at a despotic regime. U.S. Defense Secretary Donald Rumsfeld said: "[I]t's untidy. ...[F]reedom's untidy. And free people are free to make mistakes and commit crimes and do bad things."[17] Did anybody know that Donald Rumsfeld was an anarchist? I wonder—did he hold the same view during the riots in Los Angeles following the beating of Rodney King? Would he care to share his thesis about the Untidiness of Freedom with the two million people being held in U.S. prisons right now?[18] (The world's "freest" country has one of the highest numbers of prisoners per capita in the world.[19]) Would he discuss its merits with young African American men, twenty-eight percent of whom will spend some part of their adult lives in jail?[20] Could he explain why he serves under a president who oversaw one hundred and fifty-two executions when he was governor of Texas?[21]

Before the war on Iraq began, the Office of Reconstruction and Humanitarian Assistance (ORHA) sent the Pentagon a list of sixteen crucial sites to protect. The National Museum was second on that list.[22] Yet the museum was not just looted, it was desecrated. It was a repository of an ancient cultural heritage. Iraq as we know it today was part of the river valley of Mesopotamia. The civilization that grew along the banks of the Tigris and the Euphrates produced the world's first writing, first calendar, first library, first city, and, yes, the world's first democracy. King Hammurabi of Babylon was the first to codify laws governing the social life of citizens.[23] It was a code in which abandoned women, prostitutes, slaves, and even animals had rights. The Hammurabi code is acknowledged not just as the birth of legality, but the beginning of an understanding of the concept of social justice. The U.S. government could not have chosen a more inappropriate land in which to stage its illegal war and display its grotesque disregard for justice.

At a Pentagon briefing during the days of looting, Secretary Rumsfeld, Prince of Darkness, turned on his media cohorts who had served him so loyally through the war. "The images you are seeing on television, you are seeing over and over and over, and it's the same picture, of some person walking out of some building with a vase. And you see it twenty times. And you think, 'My goodness, were there that many vases? Is it possible that there were that many vases in the whole country?' "[24]

Laughter rippled through the press room. Would it be all right for the poor of Harlem to loot the Metropolitan Museum? Would it be greeted with similar mirth?

The last building on the ORHA list of sixteen sites to be protected was the Ministry of Oil.[25] It was the only one that was given adequate protection.[26] Perhaps the occupying army thought that in Muslim countries lists are read upside down?

Television tells us that Iraq has been "liberated" and that Afghanistan is well on its way to becoming a paradise for women—thanks to Bush and Blair, the twenty-first century's leading feminists. In reality, Iraq's infrastructure has been destroyed. Its people brought to the brink of starvation. Its food

Instant-Mix Imperial Democracy

stocks depleted. And its cities devastated by a complete administrative breakdown. Iraq is being ushered in the direction of a civil war between Shias and Sunnis. Meanwhile, Afghanistan has lapsed back into the pre-Taliban era of anarchy, and its territory has been carved up into fiefdoms by hostile warlords.[27]

Undaunted by all this, on May 2, 2003, Bush the Lesser launched his 2004 campaign hoping to be finally elected U.S. president. In what probably constitutes the shortest flight in history, a military jet landed on an aircraft carrier, the U.S.S. *Abraham Lincoln,* which was so close to shore that, according to the Associated Press, administration officials "acknowledged positioning the massive ship to provide the best TV angle for Bush's speech, with the vast sea as his background instead of the very visible San Diego coastline."[28] President Bush, who never served his term in the military,[29] emerged from the cockpit in fancy dress—a U.S. military bomber jacket, combat boots, flying goggles, helmet. Waving to his cheering troops, he officially proclaimed victory over Iraq. He was careful to say that it was just "one victory in a war on terror... [which] still goes on."[30]

It was important to avoid making a straightforward victory announcement, because under the Geneva Convention a victorious army is bound by the legal obligations of an occupying force, a responsibility that the Bush administration does not want to burden itself with.[31] Also, closer to the 2004 elections, in order to woo wavering voters, another victory in the "War on Terror" might become necessary. Syria is being fattened for the kill.

It was Hermann Goering, that old Nazi, who said, "People can always be brought to the bidding of the leaders. ... All you have to do is tell them they're being attacked and denounce the pacifists for a lack of patriotism and exposing the country to danger. It works the same way in any country."[32]

He's right. It's dead easy. That's what the Bush regime banks on. The distinction between election campaigns and war, between democracy and oligarchy, seems to be closing fast.

The only caveat in these campaign wars is that U.S. lives must not be lost. It shakes voter confidence. But the problem of U.S. soldiers being killed in combat has been licked. More or less.

At a media briefing before Operation Shock and Awe was unleashed, General Tommy Franks announced, "This campaign will be like no other in history."[33] Maybe he's right.

I'm no military historian, but when was the last time a war was fought like this?

As soon as the war began, the governments of France, Germany, and Russia, which refused to allow a final resolution legitimizing the war to be passed in the U.N. Security Council, fell over each other to say how much they wanted the United States to win. President Jacques Chirac offered French airspace to the Anglo-American air force.[34] U.S. military bases in Germany were open for business.[35] German foreign minister Joschka Fischer publicly hoped that Saddam Hussein's regime would "collapse as soon as possible."[36] Vladimir Putin publicly hoped for the same.[37] These are governments that colluded in the enforced disarming of Iraq before their dastardly rush to take the side of those who attacked it. Apart from hoping to share the spoils, they hoped Empire would honor their pre-war oil contracts with Iraq. Only the very naive could expect old Imperialists to behave otherwise.

Leaving aside the cheap thrills and the lofty moral speeches made in the U.N. during the run-up to the war, eventually, at the moment of crisis, the unity of Western governments—despite the opposition from the majority of their people—was overwhelming.

When the Turkish government temporarily bowed to the views of ninety percent of its population and turned down the U.S. government's offer of billions of dollars of blood money for the use of Turkish soil, it was accused of lacking "democratic credentials."[38] According to a Gallup International poll, in no European country was support for a war carried out "unilaterally by America and its allies" higher than eleven percent.[39] But the governments of England, Italy, Spain, Hungary, and other countries of Eastern Europe were praised for disregarding the views of the majority of their people and supporting the illegal invasion. That, presumably, was fully in keeping with democratic principles. What's it called? New Democracy? (Like Britain's New Labour?)

In stark contrast to the venality displayed by their governments, on February 15, 2003, weeks before the invasion, in the most spectacular display of public morality the world has ever seen, more than ten million people marched against the war on five continents.[40] Many of you, I'm sure, were among them. They—we—were disregarded with utter disdain. When asked to react to the anti-war demonstrations, President Bush said, "It's like deciding, well, I'm going to decide policy based upon a focus group. The role of a leader is to decide policy based upon the security, in this case, the security of the people."[41]

Democracy, the modern world's holy cow, is in crisis. And the crisis is a profound one. Every kind of outrage is being committed in the name of democracy. It has become little more than a hollow word, a pretty shell, emptied of all content or meaning. It can be whatever you want it to be. Democracy is the Free World's whore, willing to dress up, dress down, willing to satisfy a whole range of tastes, available to be used and abused at will.

Until quite recently, right up to the 1980s, democracy did seem as though it might actually succeed in delivering a degree of real social justice.

Instant-Mix Imperial Democracy

But modern democracies have been around for long enough for neo-liberal capitalists to learn how to subvert them. They have mastered the technique of infiltrating the instruments of democracy—the "independent" judiciary, the "free" press, the parliament—and molding them to their purpose. The project of corporate globalization has cracked the code. Free elections, a free press, and an independent judiciary mean little when the free market has reduced them to commodities on sale to the highest bidder.

To fully comprehend the extent to which democracy is under siege, it might be an idea to look at what goes on in some of our contemporary democracies. The world's largest: India, (which I have written about at some length and, therefore, will not speak about tonight). The world's most interesting: South Africa. The world's most powerful: the United States of America. And, most instructive of all, the plans that are being made to usher in the world's newest: Iraq.

In South Africa, after three hundred years of brutal domination of the black majority by a white minority through colonialism and apartheid, a nonracial, multi-party democracy came to power in 1994. It was a phenomenal achievement. Within two years of coming to power, the African National Congress had genuflected with no caveats to the Market God. Its massive program of structural adjustment, privatization, and liberalization has only increased the hideous disparities between the rich and the poor. Official unemployment among blacks has increased from forty percent to fifty percent since the end of apartheid.[42] The corporatization of basic services—electricity, water, and housing—has meant that ten million South Africans, almost a quarter of the population, have been disconnected from water and electricity.[43] Two million have been evicted from their homes.

Meanwhile, a small white minority that has been historically privileged by centuries of brutal exploitation is more secure than ever before. They continue to control the land, the farms, the factories, and the abundant natural resources of that country. For them, the transition from apartheid to neo-liberalism barely disturbed the grass. It's apartheid with a clean conscience. And it goes by the name of democracy.

Democracy has become Empire's euphemism for neo-liberal capitalism.

In countries of the first world, too, the machinery of democracy has been effectively subverted. Politicians, media barons, judges, powerful corporate lobbyists, and government officials are imbricated in an elaborate underhand configuration that completely undermines the lateral arrangement of checks and balances between the constitution, courts of law, parliament, the administration, and, perhaps most important of all, the independent media that form the structural basis of a

Instant-Mix Imperial Democracy

parliamentary democracy. Increasingly, the imbrication is neither subtle nor elaborate.

Italian Prime Minister Silvio Berlusconi, for instance, has a controlling interest in major Italian newspapers, magazines, television channels, and publishing houses. The *Financial Times* reported that he controls about ninety percent of Italy's TV viewership.[44] Recently, during a trial on bribery charges, while insisting he was the only person who could save Italy from the left, he said, "How much longer do I have to keep living this life of sacrifices?"[45] That bodes ill for the remaining ten percent of Italy's TV viewership. What price free speech? Free speech for whom?

In the United States, the arrangement is more complex. Clear Channel Communications is the largest radio station owner in the country. It runs more than twelve hundred channels, which together account for nine percent of the market.[46] When hundreds of thousands of American citizens took to the streets to protest against the war on Iraq, Clear Channel organized pro-war patriotic "Rallies for America" across the country.[47] It used its radio stations to advertise the events and then sent correspondents to cover them as though they were breaking news. The era of manufacturing consent has given way to the era of manufacturing news. Soon media newsrooms will drop the pretense, and start hiring theater directors instead of journalists.

Arundhati Roy

As America's show business gets more and more violent and warlike, and America's wars get more and more like show business, some interesting crossovers are taking place. The designer who built the $250,000 set in Qatar from which General Tommy Franks stage-managed news coverage of Operation Shock and Awe also built sets for Disney, MGM, and *Good Morning America*.[48]

It is a cruel irony that the United States, which has the most ardent, vociferous defenders of the idea of free speech, and (until recently) the most elaborate legislation to protect it, has so circumscribed the space in which that freedom can be expressed. In a strange, convoluted way, the sound and fury that accompanies the legal and conceptual defense of free speech in America serve to mask the process of the rapid erosion of the possibilities of actually exercising that freedom.

The news and entertainment industry in the United States is for the most part controlled by a few major corporations—AOL-Time Warner, Disney, Viacom, News Corporation.[49] Each of these corporations owns and controls TV stations, film studios, record companies, and publishing ventures. Effectively, the exits are sealed.

America's media empire is controlled by a tiny coterie of people. Chairman of the Federal Communications Commission Michael Powell, the son of Secretary of State Colin Powell, has proposed even further deregulation of the communications industry, which will lead to even greater consolidation.[50]

So here it is—the world's greatest democracy, led by a man who was not legally elected. America's Supreme Court gifted him his job. What price have American people paid for this spurious presidency?

In the three years of George Bush the Lesser's term, the American economy has lost more than two million jobs.[51] Outlandish military expenses, corporate welfare, and tax giveaways to the rich have created a financial crisis for the U.S. educational system. According to a survey by the National Conference of State Legislatures, U.S. states cut forty-nine billion dollars in public services, health, welfare benefits, and education in 2002. They plan to cut another $25.7 billion this year.[52] That makes a total of seventy-five billion dollars. Bush's initial budget request to Congress to finance the war in Iraq was eighty billion dollars.[53]

So who's paying for the war? America's poor. Its students, its unemployed, its single mothers, its hospital and home-care patients, its teachers, and its health workers.

And who's actually fighting the war?

Once again, America's poor. The soldiers who are baking in Iraq's desert sun are not the children of the rich. Only one of all the representatives in Congress and the Senate has a child fighting in Iraq.[54] America's "volunteer" army in fact depends on a poverty draft of poor whites, Blacks, Latinos, and Asians looking for a way to earn a living and get an education. Federal statistics show that African Americans make up twenty-one percent of the total armed forces and twenty-nine percent of the U.S. Army. They account for only twelve percent of the general population.[55] It's ironic, isn't it—the disproportionately high representation of African Americans in the army and prison? Perhaps we should take a positive view and look at this as affirmative action at its most effective. Nearly four million Americans (two percent of the population) have lost the right to vote because of felony convictions.[56] Of that number, 1.4 million are African Americans, which means that thirteen percent of all voting-age Black people have been disenfranchised.[57]

For African Americans there's also affirmative action in death. A study by the economist Amartya Sen shows that African Americans as a group have a lower life expectancy than people born in China, in the Indian State of Kerala (where I come from), Sri Lanka, or Costa Rica.[58] Bangladeshi men have a better chance of making it to the age of sixty-five than African American men from here in Harlem.[59]

This year, on what would have been Martin Luther King Jr.'s seventy-fourth birthday, President Bush denounced the University of Michigan's affirmative action program favoring Blacks and Latinos. He called it "divisive," "unfair," and unconstitutional.[60] The successful effort to keep Blacks off the voting rolls in the state of Florida in order that George Bush be elected was of course neither unfair nor unconstitutional. I don't suppose affirmative action for White Boys From Yale ever is.

So we know who's paying for the war. We know who's fighting it. But who will benefit from it? Who is homing in on the reconstruction contracts estimated to be worth up to one hundred billion dollars?[61] Could it be America's poor and unemployed and sick? Could it be America's single mothers? Or America's Black and Latino minorities?

Consider this: The Defense Policy Board advises the Pentagon on defense policy. Its members are appointed by the Under Secretary of Defense and approved by Donald Rumsfeld. Its meetings are classified. No information is available for public scrutiny.

The Washington-based Center for Public Integrity found that nine out of the thirty members of the Defense Policy Board are connected to companies that were awarded defense contracts worth seventy-six billion dollars between the years 2001 and 2002.[62] One of them, Jack Sheehan, a retired Marine Corps general, is a senior vice president at Bechtel, the giant international engineering outfit.[63] Riley Bechtel, the company chairman, is on the President's Export Council.[64] Former Secretary of State George Shultz, who is also on the board of directors of the Bechtel Group, is the chairman of the advisory board of the Committee for the Liberation of Iraq.[65] When asked by the *New York Times* whether he was concerned about the appearance of a conflict of interest, he said, "I don't know that Bechtel would particularly benefit from it. But if there's work to be done, Bechtel is the type of company that could do it."[66]

Bechtel has been awarded a $680 million reconstruction contract in Iraq.[67] According to the Center for Responsive Politics, Bechtel contributed $1.3 million toward the 1999–2000 Republican campaign.[68]

Arcing across this subterfuge, dwarfing it by the sheer magnitude of its malevolence, is America's anti-terrorism legislation. The U.S.A. Patriot Act, passed on October 12, 2001, has become the blueprint for similar anti-terrorism bills in countries across the world. It was passed in the U.S. House of Representatives by a majority vote of 337 to 79. According to the *New York Times,* "Many lawmakers said it had been impossible to truly debate, or even read, the legislation."[69]

The Patriot Act ushers in an era of systemic automated surveillance. It gives the government the authority to monitor phones and computers and spy on people in ways that would have seemed completely unacceptable a few years ago.[70] It gives the FBI the power to seize all of the circulation, purchasing, and other records of library users and bookstore customers on the suspicion that they are part of a terrorist network.[71] It blurs the boundaries between speech and criminal activity, creating the space to construe acts of civil disobedience as violating the law.

Already hundreds of people are being held indefinitely as "unlawful combatants."[72] (In India, the number is also in the hundreds.[73] In Israel, five thousand Palestinians are now being detained.[74]) Noncitizens, of course, have no rights at all. They can simply be "disappeared" like the people of Chile under Washington's old ally, General Pinochet. More than one thousand people, many of them Muslim or of Middle Eastern origin, have been detained, some without access to legal representatives.[75]

Apart from paying the actual economic costs of war, American people are paying for these wars of "liberation" with their own freedoms. For the ordinary American, the price of New Democracy in other countries is the death of real democracy at home.

Meanwhile, Iraq is being groomed for "liberation." (Or did they mean "liberalization" all along?) The *Wall Street Journal* reports that "the Bush administration has drafted sweeping plans to remake Iraq's economy in the U.S. image."[76]

Iraq's constitution is being redrafted. Its trade laws, tax laws, and intellectual property laws rewritten in order to turn it into an American-style capitalist economy.[77]

The United States Agency for International Development has invited U.S. companies to bid for contracts that range from road building and water systems to textbook distribution and cell-phone networks.[78]

Soon after Bush the Second announced that he wanted American farmers to feed the world, Dan Amstutz, a former senior executive of Cargill, the biggest grain exporter in the world, was put in charge of agricultural reconstruction in Iraq. Kevin Watkin, Oxfam's policy director, said, "Putting Dan Amstutz in charge of agricultural reconstruction in Iraq is like putting Saddam Hussein in the chair of a human rights commission."[79]

The two men who have been shortlisted to run operations for managing Iraqi oil have worked with Shell, BP, and Fluor. Fluor is embroiled in a lawsuit by black South African workers who have accused the company of exploiting and brutalizing them during the apartheid era.[80] Shell, of course, is well known for its devastation of the Ogoni tribal lands in Nigeria.[81]

Tom Brokaw (one of America's best-known TV anchors) was inadvertently succinct about the process. "One of the things we don't want to do," he said, "is to destroy the infrastructure of Iraq because in a few days we're going to own that country."[82]

Now that the ownership deeds are being settled, Iraq is ready for New Democracy.

Instant-Mix Imperial Democracy

So, as Lenin used to ask: What Is To Be Done?

Well…

We might as well accept the fact that there is no conventional military force that can successfully challenge the American war machine. Terrorist strikes only give the U.S. government an opportunity that it is eagerly awaiting to further tighten its stranglehold. Within days of an attack you can bet that Patriot II would be passed. To argue against U.S. military aggression by saying that it will increase the possibilities of terrorist strikes is futile. It's like threatening Brer Rabbit that you'll throw him into the bramble bush. Anybody who has read the document called "The Project for the New American Century" can attest to that. The government's suppression of the congressional Joint Inquiry into Intelligence Community Activities before and after the Terrorist Attacks of September 11, 2001, which found that there was intelligence warning of the strikes that was ignored,[83] also attests to the fact that, for all their posturing, the terrorists and the Bush regime might as well be working as a team. They both hold people responsible for the actions of their governments. They both believe in the doctrine of collective guilt and collective punishment. Their actions benefit each other greatly.

The U.S. government has already displayed in no uncertain terms the range and extent of its capability for paranoid aggression. In human psychology, paranoid aggression is usually an indicator of nervous insecurity. It could be argued that it's no different in the case of the psychology of nations. Empire is paranoid because it has a soft underbelly.

Its homeland may be defended by border patrols and nuclear weapons, but its economy is strung out across the globe. Its economic outposts are exposed and vulnerable.

Yet it would be naive to imagine that we can directly confront Empire. Our strategy must be to isolate Empire's working parts and disable them one by one. No target is too small. No victory too insignificant. We could reverse the idea of the economic sanctions imposed on poor countries by Empire and its Allies. We could impose a regime of Peoples' Sanctions on every corporate house that has been awarded a contract in post-war Iraq, just as activists in this country and around the world targeted institutions of apartheid. Each one of them should be named, exposed, and boycotted. Forced out of business. That could be our response to the Shock and Awe campaign. It would be a great beginning.

Another urgent challenge is to expose the corporate media for the boardroom bulletin that it really is. We need to create a universe of alternative information. We need to support independent media like *Democracy Now*, Alternative Radio, South End Press.

The battle to reclaim democracy is going to be a difficult one. Our freedoms were not granted to us by any governments. They were wrested from them by us. And once we surrender them, the battle to retrieve them is called a revolution. It is a battle that must range across continents and countries. It must not acknowledge national boundaries, but if it is to succeed, it has to begin here. In America. The only institution more powerful than the U.S. government is American civil society. The rest of us are subjects of slave nations. We are by no means powerless, but you have the power of proximity. You have access to the Imperial Palace and the Emperor's chambers. Empire's conquests are being carried out in your name, and you have the right to refuse. You could refuse to fight. Refuse to move those missiles from the warehouse to the dock. Refuse to wave that flag. Refuse the victory parade.

You have a rich tradition of resistance. You need only read Howard Zinn's *A People's History of the United States* to remind yourself of this.[84]

Hundreds of thousands of you have survived the relentless propaganda you have been subjected to, and are actively fighting your own government. In the ultra-patriotic climate that prevails in the United States, that's as brave as any Iraqi or Afghan or Palestinian fighting for his or her homeland.

If you join the battle, not in your hundreds of thousands, but in your millions, you will be greeted joyously by the rest of the world. And you will see how beautiful it is to be gentle instead of brutal, safe instead of scared. Befriended instead of isolated. Loved instead of hated.

I hate to disagree with your president. Yours is by no means a great nation. But you could be a great people.

History is giving you the chance.

Seize the time.

WHEN THE SAINTS GO MARCHING OUT

The Strange Fate of
Martin, Mohandas, and Mandela

We're coming up to the fortieth anniversary of the March on Washington, when Martin Luther King gave his famous "I have a dream" speech. Perhaps it's time to reflect—again—on what has become of that dream.

It's interesting how icons, when their time has passed, are commodified and appropriated (some voluntarily, others involuntarily) to promote the prejudice, bigotry, and inequity they battled against. But then in an age when everything's up for sale, why not icons? In an era when all of humanity, when every creature of God's earth, is trapped between the IMF

This text is an expanded version of an essay originally broadcast by BBC Radio 4, August 25, 2003. By request of the BBC, which had determined that copyright restrictions prohibited it from broadcasting direct quotations from King's public speeches, the original used only paraphrases of King's words. In this version, direct quotations have been used.

checkbook and the American cruise missile, can icons stage a getaway?

Martin Luther King is part of a trinity. So it's hard to think of him without two others elbowing their way into the picture: Mohandas Gandhi and Nelson Mandela. The three high priests of nonviolent resistance. Together they represent (to a greater or lesser extent) the twentieth century's nonviolent liberation struggles (or should we say "negotiated settlements"?): of colonized against colonizer, former slave against slave owner.

Today the elites of the very societies and peoples in whose name the battles for freedom were waged use them as mascots to entice new masters.

Mohandas, Mandela, Martin.

India, South Africa, the United States.

Broken dreams, betrayal, nightmares.

A quick snapshot of the supposedly "Free World" today.

Last March in India, in Gujarat—Gandhi's Gujarat—right-wing Hindu mobs murdered two thousand Muslims in a chillingly efficient orgy of violence. Women were gang-raped and burned alive. Muslim tombs and shrines were razed to the ground. More than a hundred and fifty thousand Muslims have been driven from their homes. The economic base of the community has been destroyed. Eyewitness accounts and several fact-finding commissions have accused the state government and the police of collusion in the violence.[1] I was present at a meeting where a group of victims kept wailing, "Please save us from the police! That's all we ask…"

In December 2002, the same state government was voted back to office. Narendra Modi, who was widely accused of having orchestrated the riots, has embarked on his second term as Chief Minister of Gujarat. On August 15, 2003, Independence Day, he hoisted the Indian flag before thousands of cheering people. In a gesture of menacing symbolism, he wore the black RSS cap—which proclaims him as a member of the Hindu nationalist guild that has not been shy of admiring Hitler and his methods.[2]

One hundred and thirty million Muslims—not to mention the other minorities, Dalits, Christians, Sikhs, Adivasis—live in India under the shadow of Hindu nationalism.

As his confidence in his political future brimmed over, Narendra Modi, master of seizing the political moment, invited Nelson Mandela to Gujarat to be the chief guest at the celebration of Gandhi's birth anniversary on October 2, 2002.[3] Fortunately the invitation was turned down.[4]

And what of Mandela's South Africa? Otherwise known as the Small Miracle, the Rainbow Nation of God? South Africans say that the only miracle they know of is how quickly the rainbow has been privatized, sectioned off, and auctioned to the highest bidders. In its rush to replace Argentina as neo-liberalism's poster child, it has instituted a massive program of privatization and structural adjustment. The government's promise to redistribute agricultural land to twenty-six million landless people has remained in the realm of dark humor.[5] While more than fifty percent of the population remains landless, almost all agricultural land is owned by sixty thousand white farmers.[6] (Small wonder that George Bush on his recent visit to South Africa referred to Thabo Mbeki as his "point man" on the Zimbabwe issue.)

Post-apartheid, the income of the poorest forty percent of Black families has diminished by about twenty percent.[7] Two million have been evicted from their homes.[8] Six hundred die of AIDS every day. Forty percent of the population is unemployed and that number is rising sharply.[9] The corporatization of basic services has meant that millions have been disconnected from water and electricity.[10]

A fortnight ago, I visited the home of Teresa Naidoo in Chatsworth, Durban. Her husband had died the previous day of AIDS. She had no money for a coffin. She and her two small children are HIV-positive. The government disconnected her water supply because she was unable to pay her water bills and her rent arrears for her tiny council flat. The government dismisses her troubles and those of millions like her as a "culture of non-payment."[11]

When the Saints Go Marching Out

In what ought to be an international scandal, this same government has officially asked the judge in a U.S. court case to rule against forcing companies to pay reparations for the role they played during apartheid.[12] Its reasoning is that reparations—in other words, justice—will discourage foreign investment.[13] So South Africa's poorest must pay apartheid's debts, so that those who amassed profit by exploiting Black people during apartheid can profit even more from the goodwill generated by Nelson Mandela's Rainbow Nation of God. President Thabo Mbeki is still called "comrade" by his colleagues in government. In South Africa, Orwellian parody goes under the genre of Real Life.

What's left to say about Martin Luther King's America? Perhaps it's worth asking a simple question: Had he been alive today, would he have chosen to stay warm in his undisputed place in the pantheon of Great Americans? Or would he have stepped off his pedestal, shrugged off the empty hosannas, and walked out on to the streets to rally his people once more?

On April 4, 1967, one year before he was assassinated, Martin Luther King spoke at the Riverside Church in New York City. That evening he said: "I could never again raise my voice against the violence of the oppressed in the ghettos without having first spoken clearly to the greatest purveyor of violence in the world today—my own government."[14]

Arundhati Roy

Has anything happened in the thirty-six years between 1967 and 2003 that would have made him change his mind? Or would he be doubly confirmed in his opinion after the overt and covert wars and acts of mass killing that successive governments of his country, both Republican and Democrat, have engaged in since then?

Let's not forget that Martin Luther King, Jr. didn't start out as a militant. He began as a Persuader, a Believer. In 1964 he won the Nobel Peace Prize. He was held up by the media as an exemplary Black leader, unlike, say, the more militant Malcolm X. It was only three years later that Martin Luther King publicly connected the U.S. government's racist war in Vietnam with its racist policies at home.

In 1967, in an uncompromising, militant speech, he denounced the American invasion of Vietnam. He said:

> [W]e have been repeatedly faced with the cruel irony of watching Negro and white boys on TV screens as they kill and die together for a nation that has been unable to seat them together in the same schools. So we watch them in brutal solidarity burning the huts of a poor village, but we realize that they would never live on the same block in Detroit.[15]

The *New York Times* had some wonderful counter-logic to offer the growing anti-war sentiment among Black Americans:

When the Saints Go Marching Out

"In Vietnam," it said, "the Negro for the first time has been given the chance to do his share of fighting for his country."[16]

It omitted to mention Martin Luther King, Jr.'s remark that "there are twice as many Negroes dying in Vietnam as whites in proportion to their size in the population."[17] It omitted to mention that when the body bags came home, some of the Black soldiers were buried in segregated graves in the Deep South.

What would Martin Luther King, Jr. say today about the fact that federal statistics show that African Americans, who account for twelve percent of America's population, make up twenty-one percent of the total armed forces and twenty-nine percent of the U.S. Army?[18]

Perhaps he would take a positive view and look at this as affirmative action at its most effective?

What would he say about the fact that having fought so hard to win the right to vote, today 1.4 million African Americans, which means thirteen percent of all voting-age Black people, have been disenfranchised because of felony convictions?[19]

To Black soldiers fighting in Vietnam, Martin Luther King, Jr. said, "As we counsel young men concerning military service we must clarify for them our nation's role in Vietnam and challenge them with the alternative of conscientious objection."[20]

Arundhati Roy

In April 1967, at a massive anti-war demonstration in Manhattan, Stokely Carmichael described the draft as "white people sending Black people to make war on yellow people in order to defend land they stole from red people."[21]

What's changed? Except of course the compulsory draft has become a poverty draft—a different kind of compulsion.

Would Martin Luther King, Jr. say today that the invasion and occupation of Iraq and Afghanistan are in any way morally different from the U.S. government's invasion of Vietnam? Would he say that it was just and moral to participate in these wars? Would he say that it was right for the U.S. government to have supported a dictator like Saddam Hussein politically and financially for years while he committed his worst excesses against Kurds, Iranians, and Iraqis—in the 1980s when he was an ally against Iran?

And that when that dictator began to chafe at the bit, as Saddam Hussein did, would he say it was right to go to war against Iraq, to fire several hundred tons of depleted uranium into its fields, to degrade its water supply systems, to institute a regime of economic sanctions that resulted in the death of half a million children, to use U.N. weapons inspectors to force it to disarm, to mislead the public about an arsenal of weapons of mass destruction that could be deployed in a matter of minutes, and then, when the country was on its knees, to send in an invading army to conquer it, occupy it, humiliate its people, take control of its natural resources and infrastructure, and award contracts worth hundreds of millions of dollars to American corporations like Bechtel?

When he spoke out against the Vietnam War, Martin Luther King, Jr. drew some connections that many these days shy away from making. He said, "[T]he problem of racism, the problem of economic exploitation, and the problem of war are all tied together. These are the triple evils that are interrelated."[22] Would he tell people today that it is right for the U.S. government to export its cruelties—its racism, its economic bullying, and its war machine—to poorer countries?

Would he say that Black Americans must fight for their fair share of the American pie and the bigger the pie, the better their share—never mind the terrible price that the people of Africa, Asia, the Middle East, and Latin America are paying for the American Way of Life? Would he support the grafting of the Great American Dream on to his own dream, which was a very different, very beautiful sort of dream? Or would he see that as a desecration of his memory and everything that he stood for?

The Black American struggle for civil rights gave us some of the most magnificent political fighters, thinkers, public speakers, and writers of our times. Martin Luther King, Jr., Malcolm X, Fannie Lou Hamer, Ella Baker, James Baldwin, and of course the marvelous, magical, mythical Muhammad Ali.

Who has inherited their mantle?

Could it be the likes of Colin Powell? Condoleezza Rice? Michael Powell?

They're the exact opposite of icons or role models. They *appear* to be the embodiment of Black people's dreams of material success, but in actual fact they represent the Great Betrayal. They are the liveried doormen guarding the portals of the glittering ballroom against the press and swirl of the darker races. Their role and purpose is to be trotted out by the Bush administration looking for brownie points in its racist wars and African safaris.

If these are Black America's new icons, then the old ones must be dispensed with because they do not belong in the same pantheon. If these are Black America's new icons, then perhaps the haunting image that Mike Marqusee describes in his beautiful book *Redemption Song*—an old Muhammad Ali, afflicted with Parkinson's disease, advertising a retirement pension—symbolizes what has happened to Black Power, not just in the United States but the world over.[23]

If Black America genuinely wishes to pay homage to its real heroes, and to all those unsung people who fought by their side, if the world wishes to pay homage, then it's time to march on Washington. Again. Keeping hope alive—for all of us.

IN MEMORY OF SHANKAR GUHA NIYOGI

We are gathered here today exactly twelve years after the murder of your beloved leader Shankar Guha Niyogi. All these years have gone by and we are still waiting for those who murdered him to be brought to justice.

I'm a writer, but in this time of urgent, necessary battle, it is important for everybody, even for writers, not usually given to public speaking, to stand before thousands of people and share their thoughts.

I am here on this very important day to say that I support and respect the spectacular struggle of the Chhattisgarh Mukti Morcha.

Yesterday, I visited the settlement around the iron-ore mines of Dalli Rajhara where the Chhattisgarh Mukti Morcha's battle began. Now it has spread across the whole of Chhattisgarh. I was deeply moved by what I saw and the people I met. What inspired me most of all was the fact that yours

---

This talk was delivered in Raipur, India, September 28, 2003, and first published in Hindi in *Hindustan* on October 13, 2003. Shankar Guha Niyogi was a popular trade union leader of Chhattisgarh.

is and always has been a struggle not just for workers' rights and farmers' rights, not just about wages and bonuses and jobs, but a struggle that has dared to dream about what it means to be human. Whenever people's rights have been assaulted, whether they are women or children, whether they are Sikhs or Muslims during communal killings, whether they are workers or farmers who were denied irrigation, you have always stood by them.

This sharp, compelling sense of humanity will have to be our weapon in times to come, when everything—our homes, our fields, our jobs, our rivers, our electricity, our right to protest, and our dignity—is being taken from us.

This is happening not just in India but in poor countries all over the world, and in response to this the poor are rising in revolt across the world.

The culmination of the process of corporate globalization is taking place in Iraq.

Imagine if you can what we would feel if thousands of armed American soldiers were patrolling the streets of India, of Chhattisgarh, deciding where we may go, who we may meet, what we must think.

It is of utmost importance that we understand that the American occupation of Iraq and the snatching away of our fields, homes, rivers, jobs, infrastructure, and resources are products of the very same process. For this reason, any strug-

In Memory of Shankar Guha Niyogi

gle against corporate globalization, any struggle for the rights and dignity of human beings must support the Iraqi people who are resisting the American occupation.

After India won independence from British rule in 1947, perhaps many of your lives did not undergo radical material change for the better. Even so, we cannot deny that it was a kind of victory, it was a kind of freedom. But today, fifty years on, even this is being jeopardized. The process of selling this country back into slavery began in the mid-1980s. The Chhattisgarh Mukti Morcha was one of the first people's resistance movements to recognize this, and so today you are an example, a beacon of light, a ray of hope for the rest of the country—and perhaps the rest of the world.

Exactly at the time when the government of India was busy undermining labor laws and dismantling the formal structures that protected workers' rights, the Chhattisgarh Mukti Morcha intensified its struggle for the rights of all workers—formal, informal, and contract laborers. For this Shankar Guha Niyogi and at least sixteen others lost their lives, killed by assassins and police bullets.[1]

When the government of India has made it clear that it is not concerned with public health, the Chhattisgarh Mukti Morcha, with contributions from workers, built the wonderful Shaheed Hospital and drew attention to the urgent necessity of providing health care to the poor.

Arundhati Roy

When the state made it clear that it was more than happy to keep the poor of India illiterate and vulnerable, the Chhattisgarh Mukti Morcha started schools for the children of workers. These schools don't just educate children, but inculcate in them revolutionary thought and create new generations of activists. Today these children led our rally, tomorrow they'll lead the resistance. It is of immense significance that this movement is led by the workers and farmers of Chhattisgarh.

To belong to a people's movement that recognized and struggled against the project of neo-imperialism as early as the Chhattisgarh Mukti Morcha did is to shoulder a great responsibility.

But you have shown, with your courage, your wisdom, and your perseverance that you are more than equal to this task. You know better than me that the road ahead is long and hard.

As a writer, as a human being, I salute you.

Lal Johar.

DO TURKEYS ENJOY THANKSGIVING?

Last January thousands of us from across the world gathered in Porto Alegre in Brazil and declared—reiterated—that "Another World Is Possible." A few thousand miles north, in Washington, George Bush and his aides were thinking the same thing.

Our project was the World Social Forum. Theirs, to further what many call "The Project for the New American Century."[1]

In the great cities of Europe and America, where a few years ago these things would only have been whispered, now people are openly talking about the good side of imperialism and the need for a strong empire to police an unruly world. The new missionaries want order at the cost of justice. Discipline at the cost of dignity. And ascendancy at any price. Occasionally some of us are invited to "debate" the issue on "neutral" platforms provided by the corporate media. De-

This speech was delivered at the World Social Forum in Bombay, India, on January 14, 2004.

bating imperialism is a bit like debating the pros and cons of rape. What can we say? That we really miss it?

In any case, New Imperialism is already upon us. It's a re-modeled, streamlined version of what we once knew. For the first time in history, a single empire with an arsenal of weapons that could obliterate the world in an afternoon has complete, unipolar, economic and military hegemony. It uses different weapons to break open different markets. Argentina's the model if you want to be the poster child of neo-liberal capital-ism, Iraq if you're the black sheep.

Poor countries that are geopolitically of strategic value to empire, or have a "market" of any size, or infrastructure that can be privatized, or, god forbid, natural resources of value—oil, gold, diamonds, cobalt, coal—must do as they're told or become military targets. Those with the greatest re-serves of natural wealth are most at risk. Unless they surrender their resources willingly to the corporate machine, civil unrest will be fomented, or war will be waged. In this new age of em-pire, when nothing is as it appears to be, executives of con-cerned companies are allowed to influence foreign policy decisions.

This brutal blueprint has been used over and over again, across Latin America, Africa, Central and Southeast Asia. It has cost millions of lives. It goes without saying that every war empire wages becomes a just war. This, in large part, is due to

Do Turkeys Enjoy Thanksgiving?

the role of the corporate media. It's important to understand that the corporate media doesn't just support the neo-liberal project. It *is* the neo-liberal project. This is not a moral position it has chosen to take, it's structural. It's intrinsic to the economics of how the mass media works.

Most nations have adequately hideous family secrets. So it isn't often necessary for the media to lie. It's all in the editing—what's emphasized and what's ignored. Say, for example, India was chosen as the target for a righteous war. The fact that about eighty thousand people have been killed in Kashmir since 1989, most of them Muslim, most of them by Indian security forces (making the average death toll about six thousand a year); the fact that in March of 2003, more than two thousand Muslims were murdered on the streets of Gujarat, that women were gang-raped and children were burned alive and a one hundred and fifty thousand people were driven from their homes while the police and administration watched, and sometimes actively participated; the fact that no one has been punished for these crimes and the government that oversaw them was re-elected...all of this would make perfect headlines in international newspapers in the run-up to war.

Next we know, our cities will be leveled by cruise missiles, our villages fenced in with razor wire, U.S. soldiers will patrol our streets, and Narendra Modi, Pravin Togadia, or any of our popular bigots could, like Saddam Hussein, be in U.S. custody, having their hair checked for lice and the fillings in their teeth examined on prime-time TV.

But as long as our "markets" are open, as long as corporations like Enron, Bechtel, Halliburton, Arthur Andersen are given a free hand, our "democratically elected" leaders can fearlessly blur the lines between democracy, majoritarianism, and fascism.

Our government's craven willingness to abandon India's proud tradition of being non-aligned, its rush to fight its way to the head of the queue of the completely aligned (the fashionable phrase is "natural ally"—India, Israel, and the United States are "natural allies"), has given it the legroom to turn into a repressive regime without compromising its legitimacy.

A government's victims are not only those whom it kills and imprisons. Those who are displaced and dispossessed and sentenced to a lifetime of starvation and deprivation must count among them too. Millions of people have been dispossessed by "development" projects.

In the era of the War against Terror, poverty is being slyly conflated with terrorism. In the era of corporate globalization, poverty is a crime. Protesting against further impoverishment is terrorism. And now, the Indian Supreme Court says that going on strike is a crime.[2] Criticizing the court of course is a crime, too.[3] They're sealing the exits.

Do Turkeys Enjoy Thanksgiving?

Like Old Imperialism, New Imperialism too relies for its success on a network of agents—corrupt local elites who service empire. We all know the sordid story of Enron in India. The then Maharashtra government signed a power purchase agreement that gave Enron profits that amounted to sixty percent of India's entire rural development budget. A single American company was guaranteed a profit equivalent to funds for infrastructural development for about five hundred million people!

Unlike in the old days, the New Imperialist doesn't need to trudge around the tropics risking malaria or diarrhea or early death. New Imperialism can be conducted on e-mail. The vulgar, hands-on racism of Old Imperialism is outdated. The cornerstone of New Imperialism is New Racism.

The tradition of "turkey pardoning" in the United States is a wonderful allegory for New Racism. Every year since 1947, the National Turkey Federation has presented the U.S. president with a turkey for Thanksgiving. Every year, in a show of ceremonial magnanimity, the president spares that particular bird (and eats another one). After receiving the presidential pardon, the Chosen One is sent to Frying Pan Park in Virginia to live out its natural life. The rest of the fifty million turkeys raised for Thanksgiving are slaughtered and eaten on Thanksgiving Day. ConAgra Foods, the company that has won the Presidential Turkey contract, says it trains the lucky birds to be sociable, to interact with dignitaries, school children, and the press. (Soon they'll even speak English!)

That's how New Racism in the corporate era works. A few carefully bred turkeys—the local elites of various countries, a community of wealthy immigrants, investment bankers, the occasional Colin Powell or Condoleezza Rice, some singers, some writers (like myself)—are given absolution and a pass to Frying Pan Park. The remaining millions lose their jobs, are evicted from their homes, have their water and electricity connections cut, and die of AIDS. Basically they're for the pot. But the Fortunate Fowls in Frying Pan Park are doing fine. Some of them even work for the IMF and the WTO—so who can accuse those organizations of being anti-turkey? Some serve as board members on the Turkey Choosing Committee—so who can say that turkeys are against Thanksgiving? They participate in it! Who can say the poor are anti-corporate globalization? There's a stampede to get into Frying Pan Park. So what if most perish on the way?

As part of the project of New Racism we also have New Genocide. New Genocide in this new era of economic interdependence can be facilitated by economic sanctions. New Genocide means creating conditions that lead to mass death without actually going out and killing people. Denis Halliday, who was the U.N. humanitarian co-ordinator in Iraq between 1997 and 1998 (after which he resigned in disgust), used the term genocide to describe the sanctions in Iraq.[4] In Iraq the sanctions outdid Saddam Hussein's best efforts by claiming more than half a million children's lives.[5]

In the new era, apartheid as formal policy is generally considered antiquated and unnecessary. International instruments of trade and finance oversee a complex system of multilateral trade laws and financial agreements that keep the poor in their Bantustans anyway. Its whole purpose is to institutionalize inequity. Why else would it be that the United States taxes a garment made by a Bangladeshi manufacturer twenty times more than it taxes a garment made in the United Kingdom?[6] Why else would it be that countries that grow ninety percent of the world's cocoa bean produce only five percent of the world's chocolate? Why else would it be that countries that grow cocoa bean, like the Ivory Coast and Ghana, are taxed out of the market if they try and turn it into chocolate?[7] Why else would it be that rich countries that spend over a billion dollars a day on subsidies to farmers demand that poor countries like India withdraw all agricultural subsidies, including subsidized electricity? Why else would it be that after having been plundered by colonizing regimes for more than half a century, former colonies are steeped in debt to those same regimes and repay them some $382 billion a year?[8]

For all these reasons, the derailing of trade agreements at Cancún was crucial for us.[9] Though our governments try and take the credit, we know that it was the result of years of struggle by many millions of people in many, many countries. What Cancún taught us is that in order to inflict real damage and force radical change, it is vital for local resistance movements to make international alliances. From Cancún we learned the importance of globalizing resistance.

No individual nation can stand up to the project of corporate globalization on its own. Time and again we have seen that when it comes to the neo-liberal project, the heroes of our times are suddenly diminished. Extraordinary, charismatic men, giants in the opposition, when they seize power and become heads of state, they become powerless on the global stage. I'm thinking here of President Lula of Brazil. Lula was the hero of the World Social Forum (WSF) last year. This year he's busy implementing IMF guidelines, reducing pension benefits, and purging radicals from the Workers' Party. I'm thinking also of ex-president of South Africa Nelson Mandela. He instituted a program of privatization and structural adjustment, leaving millions of people homeless, jobless, and without water and electricity.

Why does this happen? There's little point in beating our breasts and feeling betrayed. Lula and Mandela are, by any reckoning, magnificent men. But the moment they cross the floor from the opposition into government they become hostage to a spectrum of threats—most malevolent among them the threat of capital flight, which can destroy any government overnight. To imagine that a leader's personal charisma and a résumé of struggle will dent the corporate cartel is to have no understanding of how capitalism works, or for that matter how power works. Radical change will not be negotiated by governments; it can only be enforced by people.

At the WSF, some of the best minds in the world come together to exchange ideas about what is happening around us. These conversations refine our vision of the kind of world we're fighting for. It is a vital process that must not be undermined. However, if all our energies are diverted into this process at the cost of real political action, then the WSF, which has played such a crucial role in the movement for global justice, runs the risk of becoming an asset to our enemies. What we need to discuss urgently are strategies of resistance. We need to aim at real targets, wage real battles, and inflict real damage. Gandhi's Salt March was not just political theater. When, in a simple act of defiance, thousands of Indians marched to the sea and made their own salt, they broke the salt tax laws. It was a direct strike at the economic underpinning of the British Empire. It was *real.* While our movement has won some important victories, we must not allow nonviolent resistance to atrophy into ineffectual, feel-good political theater. It is a very precious weapon that needs to be constantly honed

and reimagined. It cannot be allowed to become a mere spectacle, a photo opportunity for the media.

It was wonderful that on February 15, 2003, in a spectacular display of public morality, ten million people in five continents marched against the war on Iraq. It was wonderful, but it
was not enough. February 15 was a weekend. Nobody had to
so much as miss a day of work. Holiday protests don't stop
wars. George Bush knows that. The confidence with which he
disregarded overwhelming public opinion should be a lesson
to us all. Bush believes that Iraq can be occupied and colonized—as Afghanistan has been, as Tibet has been, as
Chechnya is being, as East Timor once was and Palestine still
is. He thinks that all he has to do is hunker down and wait until
a crisis-driven media, having picked this crisis to the bone,
drops it, and moves on. Soon the carcass will slip off the
best-seller charts and all of us outraged folks will lose interest.
Or so he hopes.

This movement of ours needs a major, global victory. It's
not good enough to be right. Sometimes, if only in order to
test our resolve, it's important to win something. In order to
win something, we need to agree on something. That something does not need to be an overarching, preordained ideology into which we force-fit our delightfully factious,
argumentative selves. It does not need to be an unquestioning

Do Turkeys Enjoy Thanksgiving?

allegiance to one or another form of resistance to the exclusion of everything else. It could be a minimum agenda.

If all of us are indeed against imperialism and against the project of neo-liberalism, then let's turn our gaze on Iraq. Iraq is the inevitable culmination of both. Plenty of anti-war activists have retreated in confusion since the capture of Saddam Hussein. Isn't the world better off without Saddam Hussein? they ask timidly.

Let's look this thing in the eye once and for all. To applaud the U.S. Army's capture of Saddam Hussein and, therefore, in retrospect, justify its invasion and occupation of Iraq, is like deifying Jack the Ripper for disemboweling the Boston Strangler. And that after a quarter-century partnership in which the ripping and strangling was a joint enterprise. It's an in-house quarrel. They're business partners who fell out over a dirty deal. Jack's the CEO.

So, if we are against imperialism, shall we agree that we are against the U.S. occupation and that we believe that the United States must withdraw from Iraq and pay reparations to the Iraqi people for the damage that the war has inflicted?

How do we begin to mount our resistance? Let's start with something really small. The issue is not about *supporting* the resistance in Iraq against the occupation or discussing who exactly constitutes the resistance. (Are they old Killer Ba'athists, are they Islamic Fundamentalists?)

93

We have to become the global resistance to the occupation.

Our resistance has to begin with a refusal to accept the legitimacy of the U.S. occupation of Iraq. It means acting to make it materially impossible for empire to achieve its aims. It means soldiers should refuse to fight, reservists should refuse to serve, workers should refuse to load ships and aircraft with weapons. It certainly means that in countries like India and Pakistan we must block the U.S. government's plans to have Indian and Pakistani soldiers sent to Iraq to clean up after them.

I suggest we choose by some means two of the major corporations that are profiting from the destruction of Iraq. We could then list every project they are involved in. We could locate their offices in every city and every country across the world. We could go after them. We could shut them down. It's a question of bringing our collective wisdom and experience of past struggles to bear on a single target. It's a question of the desire to win.

"The Project for the New American Century" seeks to perpetuate inequity and establish American hegemony at any price, even if it's apocalyptic. The World Social Forum demands justice and survival.

For these reasons, we must consider ourselves at war.

HOW DEEP SHALL WE DIG?

Recently, a young Kashmiri friend was talking to me about life in Kashmir. Of the morass of political venality and opportunism, the callous brutality of the security forces, of the osmotic, inchoate edges of a society saturated in violence, where militants, police, intelligence officers, government servants, businessmen, and even journalists encounter each other, and gradually, over time, *become* each other. He spoke of having to live with the endless killing, the mounting "disappearances," the whispering, the fear, the unresolved rumors, the insane disconnection between what is actually happening, what Kashmiris know is happening, and what the rest of us are told is happening in Kashmir. He said, "Kashmir used to be a business. Now it's a mental asylum."

This is the full text of the first I.G. Khan Memorial Lecture, delivered at Aligarh Muslim University in Aligarh, India, on April 6, 2004. It was first published in Hindi in *Hindustan,* April 23–24, 2004, and in English in *The Hindu,* April 25, 2004. An excerpt also appeared in the *Los Angeles Times,* April 25, 2004. On the February 14, 2003, murder of I.G. Khan, see Parvathi Menon, "A Man of Compassion," *Frontline,* March 29–April 11, 2003, http://www.frontlineonnet. com/fl2007/stories/20030411004511400.htm.

The more I think about that remark, the more apposite a description it seems for all of India. Admittedly, Kashmir and the Northeast are separate wings that house the more perilous wards in the asylum. But in the heartland, too, the schism between knowledge and information, between what we know and what we're told, between what is unknown and what is asserted, between what is concealed and what is revealed, between fact and conjecture, between the "real" world and the virtual world, has become a place of endless speculation and potential insanity. It's a poisonous brew which is stirred and simmered and put to the most ugly, destructive, political purpose.

Each time there is a so-called terrorist strike, the government rushes in, eager to assign culpability with little or no investigation. The burning of the Sabarmati Express in Godhra, the December 13, 2001, attack on the parliament building, or the massacre of Sikhs by so-called terrorists in Chittisinghpura in March 2000 are only a few high-profile examples. (The so-called terrorists who were later killed by security forces turned out to be innocent villagers. The state government subsequently admitted that fake blood samples were submitted for DNA testing.[1]) In each of these cases, the evidence that eventually surfaced raised very disturbing questions and so was immediately put into cold storage. Take the case of Godhra: As soon as it happened the Home Minister announced it was an ISI plot. The VHP says it was the work of a Muslim mob throwing petrol bombs.[2] Serious questions remain unanswered. There is endless conjecture. Everybody believes what they want to believe, but the incident is used to cynically and systematically whip up communal frenzy.

The U.S. government used the lies and disinformation generated around the September 11 attacks to invade not just one country, but two—and heaven knows what else is in store.

The Indian government uses the same strategy not with other countries, but against its own people.

Over the last decade, the number of people who have been killed by the police and security forces runs into the thousands. Recently several Bombay policemen spoke openly to the press about how many "gangsters" they had eliminated on "orders" from their senior officers.[3] Andhra Pradesh chalks up an average of about two hundred "extremists" in "encounter" deaths a year.[4] In Kashmir in a situation that almost amounts to war, an estimated eighty thousand people have been killed since 1989. Thousands have simply "disappeared."[5] According to the records of the Association of Parents of Disappeared People (APDP), more than three thousand people were killed in 2003, of which four hundred and sixty-three were soldiers.[6] Since the Mufti Mohammed Sayeed government came to power in October 2002 on the promise of bringing a "healing touch," the APDP says, there have been fifty-four custodial deaths.[7] In this age of hypernationalism, as long as the people who are killed are labeled gangsters, terrorists, insurgents, or extremists, their killers can strut around as crusaders in the national interest and are answerable to no one. Even if it were true (which it most certainly isn't) that every person who has been killed was in fact a gangster, terrorist, insurgent, or extremist—it only tells us there is something terribly wrong with a society that drives so many people to take such desperate measures.

The Indian state's proclivity to harass and terrorize people has been institutionalized, consecrated, by the enactment of the Prevention of Terrorism Act (POTA), which has been promulgated in ten states. A cursory reading of POTA will tell you that it is draconian and ubiquitous. It's a versatile, hold-all law that could apply to anyone—from an Al-Qaeda operative caught with a cache of explosives to an Adivasi playing his flute under a neem tree, to you or me. The genius of POTA is that it can be anything the government wants it to be. We live on the sufferance of those who govern us. In Tamil Nadu, it has been used to stifle criticism of the state government.[8] In Jharkhand thirty-two hundred people, mostly poor Adivasis accused of being Maoists have been indicted under POTA.[9] In eastern Uttar Pradesh, the act is used to clamp down on those who dare to protest about the alienation of their land and livelihood rights.[10] In Gujarat and Mumbai, it is used almost exclusively against Muslims.[11] In Gujarat after the 2002 state-assisted pogrom in which an estimated two thousand Muslims were killed and one hundred and fifty thousand driven from their homes, two hundred eighty-seven people have been accused under POTA. Of these, two hundred and eighty-six are *Muslim* and one is a Sikh![12] POTA allows confessions extracted in police custody to be admitted as judicial evidence. In effect, under the POTA regime, police torture tends to replace police investigation. It's quicker, cheaper, and ensures results. Talk of cutting back on public spending.

In March 2004, I was a member of a peoples' tribunal on POTA. Over a period of two days we listened to harrowing testimonies of what goes on in our wonderful democracy. Let me assure you that in our police stations it's everything: from people being forced to drink urine to being stripped, humiliated, given electric shocks, burned with cigarette butts, having iron rods put up their anuses to being beaten and kicked to death.

Across the country hundreds of people, including some very young children charged under POTA, have been imprisoned and are being held without bail, awaiting trial in special POTA courts that are not open to public scrutiny. A majority of those booked under POTA are guilty of one of two crimes. Either they're poor—for the most part Dalit and Adivasi. Or they're Muslim. POTA inverts the accepted dictum of criminal law: that a person is innocent until proven guilty. Under POTA you cannot get bail unless you can prove you are innocent—of a crime that you have not been formally charged with. Essentially, you have to prove you're innocent even if you're unaware of the crime you are supposed to have committed. And that applies to all of us. Technically, we are a nation waiting to be accused.

It would be naïve to imagine that POTA is being "misused." On the contrary. It is being used for precisely the reasons it was enacted. Of course, if the recommendations of the Malimath Committee are implemented, POTA will soon become redundant. The Malimath Committee recommends that in certain respects normal criminal law should be brought in line with the provisions of POTA.[13] There'll be no more criminals then. Only terrorists. It's kind of neat.

Today in Jammu and Kashmir and many northeastern states of India, the Armed Forces Special Powers Act allows not just officers but even junior commissioned officers and noncommissioned officers of the army to use force (and even kill) any person on suspicion of disturbing public order or carrying a weapon.[14] On *suspicion of!* Nobody who lives in India can harbor any illusions about what that leads to. The documentation of instances of torture, disappearances, custodial deaths, rape, and gangrape (by security forces) is enough to make your blood run cold. The fact that, despite all this, India retains its reputation as a legitimate democracy in the international community and among its own middle class is a triumph.

The Armed Forces Special Powers Act is a harsher version of the ordinance that Lord Linlithgow passed in August 15, 1942, to handle the Quit India Movement. In 1958, it was clamped on parts of Manipur, which were declared "disturbed areas." In 1965, the whole of Mizoram, then still part of Assam was declared "disturbed." In 1972, the act was extended to Tripura. By 1980, the whole of Manipur had been declared "disturbed."[15] What more evidence does anybody need to realize that repressive measures are counter-productive and only exacerbate the problem?

Juxtaposed against this unseemly eagerness to repress and eliminate people is the Indian state's barely hidden reluctance to investigate and bring to trial cases in which there is plenty of evidence: the massacre of three thousand Sikhs in Delhi in 1984 and the massacres of Muslims in Bombay in 1993 and in Gujarat in 2002 (not one conviction to date); the murder a few years ago of Chandrashekhar Prasad, former president of the Jawaharlal Nehru University student union; and the murder twelve years ago of Shankar Guha Niyogi of the Chhattisgarh Mukti Morcha are just a few examples.[16] Eyewitness accounts and masses of incriminating evidence are not enough when all of the state machinery is stacked against you.

Meanwhile, economists cheering from the pages of corporate newspapers inform us that the GDP growth rate is phenomenal, unprecedented. Shops are overflowing with consumer goods. Government storehouses are overflowing with food grain. Outside this circle of light, farmers steeped in debt are committing suicide in the hundreds. Reports of starvation and malnutrition come in from across the country. Yet the government allowed sixty-three million tons of grain to rot in its granaries.[17] Twelve million tons were exported and sold at a subsidized price the Indian government was not willing to offer the Indian poor.[18] Utsa Patnaik, the well known agricultural economist, has calculated food grain availability and food grain absorption in India for nearly a century, based on official statistics. She calculates that in the period between the early 1990s and 2001, food grain absorption has dropped to levels lower than during the World War II years, including during the Bengal Famine, in which three million people died of starvation.[19] As we know from the work of Professor Amartya Sen, democracies don't take kindly to starvation deaths. They attract too much adverse publicity from the "free press."[20] So, dangerous levels of malnutrition and permanent hunger are the preferred model these days. Forty-seven percent of India's children below three suffer from malnutrition, forty-six percent are stunted.[21] Utsa Patnaik's study reveals that about forty percent of the rural population in India has the same food

How Deep Shall We Dig?

grain absorption level as sub-Saharan Africa.[22] Today, an average rural family eats about one hundred kilograms less food in a year than it did in the early 1990s.[23]

But in urban India, wherever you go—shops, restaurants, railway stations, airports, gymnasiums, hospitals—you have TV monitors in which election promises have already come true. India's Shining, Feeling Good. You only have to close your ears to the sickening crunch of the policeman's boot on someone's ribs, you only have to raise your eyes from the squalor, the slums, the ragged broken people on the streets and seek a friendly TV monitor and you will be in that other beautiful world. The singing-dancing world of Bollywood's permanent pelvic thrusts, of permanently privileged, permanently happy Indians waving the tricolor flag and Feeling Good. It's becoming harder and harder to tell which one's the real world and which one's virtual. Laws like POTA are like buttons on a TV. You can use it to switch off the poor, the troublesome, the unwanted.

There is a new kind of secessionist movement taking place in India. Shall we call it New Secessionism? It's an inversion of Old Secessionism. It's when people who are actually part of a whole different economy, a whole different country, a whole different *planet,* pretend they're part of this one. It is the kind of secession in which a relatively small section of people become immensely wealthy by appropriating everything—

103

land, rivers, water, freedom, security, dignity, fundamental rights, including the right to protest—from a large group of people. It's a vertical secession, not a horizontal, territorial one. It's the real Structural Adjustment—the kind that separates India Shining from India. India Pvt. Ltd. from India the Public Enterprise.

It's the kind of secession in which public infrastructure, productive public assets—water, electricity, transport, telecommunications, health services, education, natural resources—assets that the Indian state is supposed to hold in trust for the people it represents, assets that have been built and maintained with public money over decades—are sold by the state to private corporations. In India seventy percent of the population—seven hundred million people—live in rural areas.[24] Their livelihoods depend on access to natural resources. To snatch these away and sell them as stock to private companies is beginning to result in dispossession and impoverishment on a barbaric scale.

India Pvt. Ltd. is on its way to being owned by a few corporations and major multinationals. The CEOs of these companies will control this country, its infrastructure and its resources, its media and its journalists, but will owe nothing to its people. They are completely unaccountable—legally, socially, morally, politically. Those who say that in India a few of these CEOs are more powerful than the Prime Minister know exactly what they're talking about.

Quite apart from the economic implications of all this, even if it were all that it is cracked up to be (which it isn't)—miraculous, efficient, amazing,—is the *politics* of it acceptable to us? If the Indian state chooses to mortgage its responsibilities to a handful of corporations, does it mean that the theater of electoral democracy is entirely meaningless? Or does it still have a role to play?

The Free Market (which is actually far from free) needs the State, and needs it badly. As the disparity between the rich and poor grows in poor countries, states have their work cut out for them. Corporations on the prowl for "sweetheart deals" that yield enormous profits cannot push through those deals and administer those projects in developing countries without the active connivance of state machinery. Today corporate globalization, needs an international confederation of loyal, corrupt, preferably authoritarian governments in poorer countries, to push through unpopular reforms, and quell the mutinies. It's called "Creating a Good Investment Climate."

When we vote, we choose which political party we would like to invest the coercive, repressive powers of the state in.

Right now in India we have to negotiate the dangerous crosscurrents of neo-liberal capitalism and communal neo-fascism. While the word capitalism hasn't completely lost its sheen yet, using the word *fascism* often causes offense. So we must ask ourselves, are we using the word loosely? Are we exaggerating our situation, does what we are experiencing on a daily basis qualify as fascism?

When a government more or less openly supports a pogrom against members of a minority community in which up to two thousand people are brutally killed, is it fascism? When women of that community are publicly raped and burned alive, is it fascism? When authorities collude to see to it that nobody is punished for these crimes, is it fascism? When one hundred and fifty thousand people are driven from their homes, ghettoized, and economically and socially boycotted, is it fascism? When the cultural guild that runs hate camps across the country commands the respect and admiration of the prime minister, the home minister, the law minister, the disinvestment minister, is it fascism? When painters, writers, scholars, and filmmakers who protest are abused, threatened, and have their work burned, banned, and destroyed, is it fascism? When a government issues an edict requiring the arbitrary alteration of school history textbooks, is it fascism? When mobs attack and burn archives of ancient historical documents, when every minor politician masquerades as a professional medieval historian and archeologist, when painstaking scholarship is rubbished using baseless populist assertion, is it fascism? When murder, rape, arson, and mob justice are

How Deep Shall We Dig?

condoned by the party in power and its stable of stock intellectuals as an appropriate response to a real or perceived historical wrong committed centuries ago, is it fascism? When the middle-class and the well-heeled pause a moment, tut-tut, and then go on with their lives, is it fascism? When the prime minister who presides over all of this is hailed as a statesman and visionary, are we not laying the foundations for full-blown fascism?

That the history of oppressed and vanquished people remains for the large part unchronicled is a truism that does not apply only to Savarna Hindus. If the politics of avenging historical wrong is our chosen path, then surely the Dalits and Adivasis of India have the right to murder, arson, and wanton destruction?

In Russia, they say the past is unpredictable. In India, from our recent experience with school history textbooks, we know how true that is. Now all "pseudo-secularists" have been reduced to hoping that archeologists digging under the Babri Masjid wouldn't find the ruins of a Ram temple. But even if it were true that there is a Hindu temple under every mosque in India, what was under the temple? Perhaps another Hindu temple to another god. Perhaps a Buddhist stupa. Most likely an Adivasi shrine. History didn't begin with Savarna Hinduism did it? How deep shall we dig? How much should we overturn? And why is it that while Muslims—who are socially, culturally, and economically an unalienable part of India—are called outsiders and invaders and are cruelly targeted, the government is busy signing corporate deals and contracts for development aid with a government that colonized us for centuries? Between 1876 and 1892, during the great famines, millions of Indians died of starvation while the British government continued to export food and raw materials to England. Historical records put the figure between twelve and twenty-nine million people.[25] That should figure somewhere in the politics of revenge, should it not? Or is vengeance only fun when its victims are vulnerable and easy to target?

Successful fascism takes hard work. And so does Creating a Good Investment Climate. Do the two work well together? Historically, corporations have not been shy of fascists. Corporations like Siemens, I.G. Farben, Bayer, IBM, and Ford did business with the Nazis.[26] We have the more recent example of our own Confederation of Indian Industry (CII) abasing itself to the Gujarat government after the pogrom in 2002.[27] As long as our markets are open, a little homegrown fascism won't come in the way of a good business deal.

It's interesting that just around the time Manmohan Singh, then the finance minister, was preparing India's markets for neo-liberalism, L.K. Advani was making his first Rath Yatra, fueling communal passion and preparing us for neo-fascism. In December 1992, rampaging mobs destroyed

How Deep Shall We Dig?

the Babri Masjid. In 1993, the Congress government of Maharashtra signed a power purchase agreement with Enron. It was the first private power project in India. The Enron contract, disastrous as it has turned out, kick-started the era of privatization in India. Now, as the Congress whines from the sidelines, the Bharatiya Janata Party (BJP) has wrested the baton from its hands.* The government is conducting an extraordinary dual orchestra. While one arm is busy selling off the nation's assets in chunks, the other, to divert attention, is arranging a baying, howling, deranged chorus of cultural nationalism. The inexorable ruthlessness of one process feeds directly into the insanity of the other.

---

* In May 2004, the right-wing BJP-led coalition was not just voted out of power, it was humiliated by the Indian electorate. None of the political pundits had predicted this decisive vote against communalism and neo-liberalism's economic "reforms." Yet even as we celebrate, we know that on every major issue other than overt Hindu nationalism—nuclear bombs, big dams, privatization—the newly elected Congress Party and the BJP have no major ideological differences. We know that it was the legacy of the Congress that led us to the horror of the BJP. Still we celebrated, because surely a darkness has passed. Or has it? Even before it formed a government, the Congress made overt reassurances that "reforms" would continue. Exactly what kind of reforms, we'll have to wait and see. Fortunately the Congress will be hobbled by the fact that it needs the support of left parties—the only parties to be overtly (if ineffectively) critical of the reforms—to make up a majority in order to form a goverment. The left parties have been given an unprecedented mandate. Hopefully, things will change. A little. It's been a pretty hellish six years.

Economically, too, the dual orchestra is a viable model. Part of the enormous profits generated by the process of indiscriminate privatization (and the accruals of "India Shining") goes into financing Hindutva's vast army—the RSS, the VHP, the Bajrang Dal, and the myriad other charities and trusts that run schools, hospitals, and social services. Between them they have tens of thousands of shakhas across the country. The hatred they preach, combined with the unmanageable frustration generated by the relentless impoverishment and dispossession of the corporate globalization project, fuels the violence of poor on poor—the perfect smoke screen to keep the structures of power intact and unchallenged.

However, directing people's frustrations into violence is not always enough. In order to Create a Good Investment Climate, the state often needs to intervene directly.

In recent years, the police has repeatedly opened fire on unarmed people, mostly Adivasis, at peaceful demonstrations. In Nagarnar, Jharkhand; in Mehndi Kheda, Madhya Pradesh; in Umergaon, Gujarat; in Rayagara and Chilika, Orissa; in Muthanga, Kerala. People are killed for encroaching on forest land, as well as when they're trying to protect forest land from dams, mining operations, steel plants.

The repression goes on and on. Jambudweep, Kashipur, Maikanj. In almost every instance of police firing, those who have been fired upon are immediately called militants.

How Deep Shall We Dig?

When victims refuse to be victims, they are called terrorists and are dealt with as such. POTA is the broad-spectrum
antibiotic for the disease of dissent. There are other, more spe-
cific steps that are being taken—court judgments that in effect
curtail free speech, the right to strike, the right to life and livelihood.

This year, one hundred and eighty-one countries voted in
the United Nations for increased protection of human rights
in the era of the War on Terror. Even the United States voted
in favor of the resolution. India abstained.[28] The stage is being
set for a full-scale assault on human rights

So how can ordinary people counter the assault of an increasingly violent state?

The space for nonviolent civil disobedience has atro-
phied. After struggling for several years, several nonviolent
people's resistance movements have come up against a wall
and feel, quite rightly, they have to now change direction.
Views about what that direction should be are deeply polar-
ized. There are some who believe that an armed struggle is the
only avenue left. Leaving aside Kashmir and the Northeast,
huge swathes of territory, whole districts in Jharkhand, Bihar,
Uttar Pradesh, and Madhya Pradesh are controlled by those
who hold that view. Others increasingly are beginning to feel
they must participate in electoral politics—enter the system,
negotiate from within. (Similar, is it not, to the choices people

111

faced in Kashmir?) The thing to remember is that while their methods differ radically, both sides share the belief that, to put it crudely, Enough is Enough. *Ya Basta.*

There is no debate taking place in India that is more crucial than this one. Its outcome will, for better or for worse, change the quality of life in this country. For everyone. Rich, poor, rural, urban.

Armed struggle provokes a massive escalation of violence from the state. We have seen the morass it has led to in Kashmir and across the Northeast.

So then, should we do what our prime minister suggests we do? Renounce dissent and enter the fray of electoral politics? Join the road show? Participate in the shrill exchange of meaningless insults which serve only to hide what is otherwise an almost absolute consensus? Let's not forget that on every major issue—nuclear bombs, big dams, the Babri Masjid controversy, and privatization—the Congress sowed the seeds and the BJP swept in to reap the hideous harvest.

This does not mean that the parliament is of no consequence and elections should be ignored. Of course there is a difference between an overtly communal party with fascist leanings and an opportunistically communal party. Of course there is a difference between a politics that openly, proudly preaches hatred and a politics that slyly pits people against each other.

How Deep Shall We Dig?

But the legacy of one has led us to the horror of the other. Between them, they have eroded any real choice that parliamentary democracy is supposed to provide. The frenzy, the fairground atmosphere created around elections, takes center stage in the media because everybody is secure in the knowledge that regardless of who wins, the status quo will essentially remain unchallenged. (After the impassioned speeches in parliament, repealing POTA doesn't seem to be a priority in any party's election campaign. They all know they need it, in one form or another.) Whatever they say during elections or when they're in the opposition, no state or national government and no political party—right, left, center, or sideways—has managed to stay the hand of neo-liberalism. There will be no radical change from "within."

Personally, I don't believe that entering the electoral fray is a path to alternative politics. Not because of that middle-class squeamishness—"politics is dirty" or "all politicians are corrupt"—but because I believe that strategically battles must be waged from positions of strength, not weakness.

The targets of the dual assault of neo-liberalism and communal fascism are the poor and the minority communities. As neo-liberalism drives its wedge between the rich and the poor, between India Shining and India, it becomes increasingly absurd for any mainstream political party to pretend to represent the interests of both the rich and the poor, because the interests of one can only be represented at the *cost* of the other. My "interests" as a wealthy Indian (were I to pursue them) would hardly coincide with the interests of a poor farmer in Andhra Pradesh.

A political party that represents the poor will be a poor party. A party with very meager funds. Today it isn't possible to fight an election without funds. Putting a couple of well-known social activists into parliament is interesting, but not really politically meaningful. Not a process worth channeling all our energies into. Individual charisma, personality politics, cannot effect radical change.

However, being poor is not the same as being weak. The strength of the poor is not indoors in office buildings and courtrooms. It's outdoors, in the fields, the mountains, the river valleys, the city streets, and university campuses of this country. That's where negotiations must be held. That's where the battle must be waged.

Right now, those spaces have been ceded to the Hindu Right. Whatever anyone might think of their politics, it cannot be denied that they're out there, working extremely hard. As the state abrogates its responsibilities and withdraws funds from health, education, and essential public services, the foot soldiers of the Sangh Parivar have moved in. Alongside their tens of thousands of shakhas disseminating deadly propaganda, they run schools, hospitals, clinics, ambulance services, disaster management cells. They understand powerlessness. They also understand that people, and particularly powerless people, have needs and desires that are not only practical, humdrum day-to-day needs, but emotional, spiritual, recreational. They have fashioned a hideous crucible into which the anger, the frustration, the indignity of daily life—and dreams of a different future—can be decanted and directed to deadly purpose. Meanwhile, the traditional, mainstream left still dreams of "seizing power," but remains strangely unbending, unwilling to address the times. It has laid siege to itself and retreated into an inaccessible intellectual space, where ancient arguments are proffered in an archaic language that few can understand.

The only ones who present some semblance of a challenge to the onslaught of the Sangh Parivar are the grassroots resistance movements scattered across the country, fighting the dispossession and violation of fundamental rights caused by our current model of "development." Most of these movements are isolated and, despite the relentless accusation that they are "foreign funded agents," work with almost no money or resources at all. They're magnificent firefighters. They have their backs to the wall. But they have their ears to the ground, and they are in touch with grim reality. If they got together, if they were supported and strengthened, they could grow into a force to reckon with. Their battle, when it is fought, will have to be an idealistic one—not a rigidly ideological one.

At a time when opportunism is everything, when hope seems lost, when everything boils down to a cynical business deal, we must find the courage to dream. To reclaim romance. The romance of believing in justice, in freedom, and in dignity. For everybody. We have to make common cause, and to do this we need to understand how this big old machine works—who it works for and who it works against. Who pays, who profits.

Many nonviolent resistance movements fighting isolated, single-issue battles across the country have realized that their kind of special interest politics, which had its time and place, is no longer enough. That they feel cornered and ineffectual is not good enough reason to abandon nonviolent resistance as a strategy. It is, however, good enough reason to do some serious introspection. We need vision. We need to make sure that those of us who say we want to reclaim democracy are egalitarian and democratic in our own methods of functioning. If our struggle is to be an idealistic one, we cannot really make caveats for the internal injustices that we perpetrate on one another, on women, on children. For example, those fighting communalism cannot turn a blind eye to economic injustices. Those fighting dams or development projects cannot elide issues of communalism or caste politics in their spheres of influence—even at the cost of short-term success in their immediate campaign. If opportunism and expediency come at the cost of our beliefs, then there is nothing to separate us from mainstream politicians. If it is justice that we want, it must be justice and equal rights for all—not only for special interest groups with special interest prejudices. That is nonnegotiable.

We have allowed nonviolent resistance to atrophy into feel-good political theater, which at its most successful is a photo opportunity for the media, and at its least successful is simply ignored.

We need to look up and urgently discuss strategies of resistance, wage real battles, and inflict real damage. We must remember that the Dandi March was not just fine political theater. It was a strike at the economic underpinning of the British Empire.

We need to redefine the meaning of politics. The "NGO-ization" of civil society initiatives is taking us in exactly the opposite direction. It's depoliticizing us. Making us dependent on aid and handouts. We need to reimagine the meaning of civil disobedience.

Perhaps we need an elected shadow parliament *outside* the Lok Sabha, without whose support and affirmation parliament cannot easily function. A shadow parliament that keeps up an underground drumbeat, that shares intelligence and information (all of which is increasingly unavailable in the mainstream media). Fearlessly, but nonviolently, we must disable the working parts of this machine that is consuming us.

We're running out of time. Even as we speak, the circle of violence is closing in. Either way, change will come. It could be bloody, or it could be beautiful. It depends on us.

GLOSSARY

Adivasi: Original inhabitants of India, literally, tribal.

Adivasi Mukti Sangathan: Activist group in Madhya Pradesh, literally, Adivasi Liberation Group.

Babri Masjid: On December 6, 1992, violent mobs of Hindu fundamentalists converged on the town of Ayodhya and demolished the Babri Masjid, an old Muslim mosque. It was the culmination of a nationwide campaign to "arouse the pride" of Hindus. Plans for replacing it with a huge Hindu temple (Ram Mandir) are under way.

Bajrang Dal: Militant Hindu fundamentalist organization named after the Hindu God Hanuman. Allied with the Bharatiya Janata Party, the Bajrang Dal, and the Vishwa Hindu Parishad (VHP), instrumental in the destruction of the Babri Masjid in Ayodhya in 1992.

Bharatiya Janata Party (BJP): Right-wing Hindu nationalist party, literally, the Indian People's Party.

Chhattisgarh Mukti Morcha: A trade union group in the mining areas of Chhattisgarh, literally, the Chhattisgarh Liberation Front.

Dalit: Those who are oppressed or literally "ground down." The preferred term for those who used to be called "untouchables" in India.

Dharna: Protest, or sit-in.

119

Hindutva: Ideology seeking to strengthen "Hindu identity" and create a Hindu state, advocated by the BJP, Shiv Sena, and other communalist parties.

ISI: Inter Services Intelligence, the Pakistani intelligence agency.

Jamadarni: A sweeper woman, usually used pejoratively.

Kinara Bachao Andolan: Activist group working in coastal Gujarat, literally, Movement to Save the Coast.

L.K. Advani: Former Indian deputy prime minister who has close associations with right-wing Hindu fundamentalist groups in India and led the Rath Yatra in 1990.

Lal Johar: Salutation of the Chhattisgarh Mukti Morcha, literally, Red Salute.

Lord Linlithgow: Governor-general of India from April 1936 to April 1943.

LTTE: Liberation Tigers of Tamil Eelam, Sri Lankan Tamil separatist guerilla group

Malimath Committee: The Committee on Reforms of the Criminal Justice System, constituted by the government of India in November 2000 and headed by retired justice V.S. Malimath, former chief justice of Kerala and Karnataka.

Mandal Commission: Commission constituted by the Janata Party Government under the chairmanship of B.P. Mandal in 1977 to look into the issue of reservations for "backward" castes in government jobs and educational institutions. The report was submitted in 1980, and its recommendations led to a huge backlash from upper castes, with violence and agitations across the country.

Mandir: Temple.

Masjid: Mosque.

Glossary

MCC: Maoist Coordination Committee, extreme left-wing armed group, present in many states in India.

Mehndi Kheda: Village in the state of Madhya Pradesh, the site of a clash between Adivasis and the police.

Muthanga: Wildlife sanctuary in the state of Kerala, the site of a clash between Adivasis and the police.

Narendra Modi: Chief minister of Gujarat; presided over the state government when violent riots took more than two thousand Muslim lives in 2002.

Narmada Bachao Andolan (NBA): Save the Narmada Movement.

Nimad Malwa Kisan Mazdoor Sangathan: Alliance of activist groups working in Madhya Pradesh on issues of water, power, and privatization of resources. Literally, the Nimad Malwa Peasants' and Workers' Organization.

Pravin Togadia: Former surgeon, rabble-rousing demagogue of the Hindu right wing, synonymous with inflammatory hate speech against Muslims.

PWG: Peoples' War Group, an extreme left-wing armed group, present in many states in India.

Ram Mandir: See Babri Masjid, above.

Rashtriya Swayamsevak Sangh (RSS): Right-wing Hindu cultural guild with a clearly articulated anti-Muslim stand and a nationalistic ideology of Hindutva. The RSS is the ideological backbone of the BJP. Literally, the National Self-Help Group.

Rath Yatra: Literally, the Chariots' Journey, a long road rally led by an ornamental bus dressed up as a chariot, undertaken first in 1990 by L.K. Advani to "mobilize Hindu sentiment" for the building of the Ram Mandir at Ayodhya. It culminated in widespread violence in many parts of northern India.

Sangh Parivar: Term used to refer to the group of closely linked right-wing Hindu fundamentalist organizations in India that includes the Bajrang Dal, BJP, RSS, and VHP. Literally, family group.

S.A.R. Geelani: Teacher of Arabic at Delhi University, implicated for being part of the conspiracy behind the attack on the Indian parliament in December 2002, and sentenced to death. He was acquitted and released after nearly two years in jail.

Savarna Hinduism: That part of caste Hindu society which excludes the Dalits and so-called backward castes.

Shankar Guha Niyogi: Trade union leader of the Chhattisgarh Mukti Morcha, killed in September 1991 by hired assassins.

Shiv Sena: Right-wing regional Hindu chauvinist party in the state of Maharashtra.

Stupa: A Buddhist religious monument.

VHP: Vishwa Hindu Parishad, literally, the World Hindu Council, self-appointed leaders of the Hindu community and part of the Sangh Parivar.

NOTES

CHAPTER 1: PEACE IS WAR

1   Mohammed Shehzad, " 'Killing Hindus' Better than Dialogue with India: Lashkar-e-Taiba Chief," *Agence France-Presse*, April 3, 2003.

2   Ben H. Bagdikian, *The New Media Monopoly* (Boston: Beacon Press, 2004).

3   Edward Helmore, "Who Sets the TV Control?: Battle Is Raging Over a Decision to Allow US Media Giants to Own Even More," *The Observer* (London), June 8, 2003, p. 6.

4   Howard Rheingold, "From the Screen to the Streets," *In These Times*, November 17, 2003, p. 34; Stephen Labaton, "Debate/Monopoly on Information: It's a World of Media Plenty: Why Limit Ownership?" *New York Times*, October 12, 2003, p. 4: 4.

5   See Connie Koch, *2/15: The Day the World Said No to War* (New York: Hello [NYC]; Oakland: AK Press, 2004).

6   See Edward Luce, "Battle Over Ayodhya Temple Looms," *Financial Times* (London), February 2, 2002, p. 7.

7   Pankaj Mishra, "A Mediocre Goddess," *New Statesman,* April 9, 2001; John Ward Anderson, "The Flame That Lit An Inferno: Hindu Leader Creates Anti-Muslim Frenzy," *Washington Post,* August 11, 1993, p. A14. See also Arundhati Roy, "Democracy: Who Is She When She Is at Home?" in

War Talk (Cambridge, MA: South End Press, 2003), pp. 17–44.

8   See Chapter 5, "In Memory of Shankar Guha Niyogi," below.

9   Raja Bose, "A River Runs Through It," *Times of India,* February 25, 2001.

10 C. Rammanohar Reddy, "At Loggerheads Over Resources," *The Hindu,* May 27, 2001; Kata Lee (Project Coordinator of Hotline Asia), "India: Unarmed Tribals Killed by Jharkhand Police," Asian Center for the Progress of Peoples (ACPP), Asian Human Rights Commission, March 3, 2003, http://www.ahrchk.net/news/mainfile.php/ahrnews_20010 3/1496/?print=yes.

11 Gurbir Singh, "Guj[arat] Police Cane Protesters of NATELCO-UNOCAL Port," *The Economic Times,* April 12, 2000; "Human Rights Defenders Persecuted in India: Amnesty [International]," The Press Trust of India, April 26, 2000. See also Rosa Basanti, "Villagers Take On Giant Port Project," Inter Press Service, June 7, 2000.

12 Sanjay Kumar, "The Adivasis of Orissa," *The Hindu,* November 6, 2001; Anu Kumar, "Orissa: A Continuing Denial of Adivasi Rights," InfoChange News and Features, November 2003, Centre for Communication and Development Studies, http://www.infochangeindia.org/ analysis10.jsp. See also "When Freedom Is Trampled Upon," *The Hindu,* January 24, 1999.

13 Danielle Knight, "The Destructive Impact of Fish Farming," Inter Press Service, October 13, 1999.

14 "Eviction of Tribals by Force in Kerala to be Taken Up with NHRC," *The Hindu,* February 26, 2003.

15 On the Nagarnar attacks, see Kuldip Nayar, "Pushing the POTO," *The Hindu,* November 28, 2001.

16 People's War Group (PWG), Maoist Communist Centre (MCC), Pakistan's Inter-Services Intelligence (ISI), and the Liberation Tigers of Tamil Eelam (LTTE).

Notes

17 "Mr. [Vakkom] Purushothaman said he was of the view that the Adivasis who had 'tried to establish a parallel government should have been suppressed or shot.'" Quoted in "Opposition Boycotts Assembly," *The Hindu,* February 22, 2003.

18 See Mari Marcel Thekaekara, "What Really Happened," *Frontline,* March 15–28, 2003, http://www.frontlineonnet.com/fl2006/stories/20030328002204600.htm.

19 Sanjay Nigam, Mangat Verma, Chittaroopa Palit, "Fifteen Thousand Farmers Gather in Mandleshwar to Protest Against Electricity Tariff Hikes in Madhya Pradesh," Nimad Malwa Kisan Mazdoor Sangathan press release, February 27, 2003, http://www.narmada.org/nba-press-releases/february-2003/antitariff.html.

20 World Commission on Dams, *Dams and Development: A New Framework for Decision-Making: The Report of the World Commission on Dams* (London and Sterling, Virginia: Earthscan, 2000), box 4.3, p. 104.

21 Arundhati Roy, *The Cost of Living* (New York: Modern Library, 1999) and *Power Politics,* 2nd ed. (Cambridge, MA: South End Press, 2001).

22 L.S. Aravinda, "Supreme Court Majority Judgment: Mockery of Modern India," Association for India's Development, http://www.aidindia.org/hq/publications/essays/articles.htm.

23 World Bank Water Resources Management Group, *The World Bank Water Resources Sector Strategy: Strategic Directions for World Bank Engagement* (Washington, D.C.: International Bank for Reconstruction and Development/World Bank, 2004), http://lnweb18.worldbank.org/ESSD/ardext.nsf/18ByDocName/Strategy; Peter Bosshard, Janneke Bruil, Carol Welch, Korinna Horta, and Shannon Lawrence, "Gambling with People's Lives: What the World Bank's New 'High-Risk/High-Reward' Strategy Means for the Poor and the Environment," September 19, 2003, http://www.

environmentaldefense.org/article.cfm?ContentID=3005. See also Carrieann Davies, "From the Editor: Back to the Future," *Water Power & Dam Construction,* April 30, 2003, p. 3.

24 "Major Rivers to Be Linked by 2016," The Press Trust of India, December 17, 2002. See also Medha Patkar, ed., *River Linking: A Millennium Folly?* (Pune, India: National Alliance of People's Movements/Initiative, 2004).

25 See "Tribals' Promised Land is Kerala Sanctuary," *Indian Express,* February 6, 2003.

26 "Call to Prosecute Grasim Management for Pollution," *Business Line,* February 1, 1999.

27 R. Krishnakumar, "Closure of Grasim Industries," *Frontline,* July 21–August 3, 2001, http://www.frontlineonnet.com/fl1 815/18151320.htm.

CHAPTER 2:
THE ORDINARY PERSON'S GUIDE TO EMPIRE

1 CNN International, March 21, 2003.

2 CNN International, March 21, 2003.

3 CNN International, March 21, 2003. See also Dexter Filkins, "In the Field Marines: Either Take a Shot or Take a Chance," *New York Times,* March 29, 2003, p. A1. Filkins interviewed Sergeant Eric Schrumpf, aged twenty-eight, of the Fifth Marine Regiment. " 'We had a great day,' Sergeant Schrumpf said. 'We killed a lot of people.'... 'We dropped a few civilians,... but what do you do?'... He recalled watching one of the women standing near the Iraqi soldier go down. 'I'm sorry,' the sergeant said. 'But the chick was in the way.' "

4 Patrick E. Tyler and Janet Elder, "Threats and Responses: The Poll: Poll Finds Most in U.S. Support Delaying a War," *New York Times,* February 14, 2003, p. A1.

5 Maureen Dowd, "The Xanax Cowboy," *New York Times,* March 9, 2003, p. 4: 13.

Notes

6   George W. Bush, joint statement with Tony Blair after the Azores summit. See "Excerpts From Remarks by Bush and Blair: 'Iraq Will Soon Be Liberated,'" *New York Times,* April 9, 2003, p. B7.

7   "You Cannot Hide, Hoon Tells Saddam," *Birmingham Evening Mail,* March 20, 2003, p. 2. Charles Reiss "We Had No Option But to Use Force to Disarm Saddam, Says Straw," *The Evening Standard* (London), March 20, 2003, p. 11.

8   General Vince Brooks, deputy director of operations, United States Central Command Daily Press Briefing, Federal News Service, March 27, 2003.

9   CNN International, March 25, 2003.

10   Remarks by President George W. Bush to Troops at MacDill Air Force Base, Tampa, Florida, Federal News Service, March 26, 2003.

11   See David Cole, *Enemy Aliens: Double Standards and Constitutional Freedoms in the War on Terrorism* (New York: The New Press, 2003).

12   Charles Lane, "Justices to Rule on Detainees' Rights; Court Access for 660 Prisoners at Issue," *Washington Post,* November 11, 2003, p. 1; David Rohde, "U.S. Rebuked on Afghans in Detention," *New York Times,* March 8, 2004, p. A6. See also Cole, *Enemy Aliens,* pp. 39–45.

13   Jeremy Armstrong, "Field of Death: Total Slaughter: Amnesty [International] Demands Probe Be Over Bloody Massacre of Taliban Prisoners," *The Mirror* (London), November 29, 2001, p. 6.

14   "Injustice in Afghanistan," editorial, *Washington Post,* March 21, 2004, p. B6.

15   Bill O'Reilly, "Talking Points Memo," *The O'Reilly Factor,* Fox News, March 24, 2003. See also Bill O'Reilly, "Unresolved Problems: Interview with Kenneth Roth," *The O'Reilly Factor,* Fox News, March 27, 2003.

16   See Rageh Omaar, *Revolution Day: The Human Story of the Battle for Iraq* (London: Viking, 2004).

17   Martin Bright, Ed Vulliamy, and Peter Beaumont, "Revealed: US Dirty Tricks to Win Vote on Iraq War," *The Observer* (London), March 2, 2003, p. 1.

18   Marc Santora, "Aid Workers Fear Dangers of Delay: Basra, Without Power and Water, Is at Risk," *International Herald Tribune,* March 25, 2003, p. 1; John Pilger, "Gulf War 2: Six Days of Shame," *The Mirror* (London), March 26, 2003, p. 14.

19   Patrick Nicholson, "The Cans and Buckets Are Empty and People Are Desperate," *The Independent* (London), April 5, 2003, p. 8.

20   Agence France-Presse, "Iraq's Weekly Oil Production Reaches New Levels," July 23, 2002.

21   Mark Nicholson, "Troops Prepare to Deliver Supplies," *Financial Times* (London), March 27, 2003, p. 2.

22   Nick Guttmann, "Humanitarian Aid: Wanted: 32 Galahads a Day," *Independent on Sunday* (London), March 30, 2003, p. 26.

23   Quoted in Noam Chomsky, *For Reasons of State* (New York: New Press, 2003), pp. 67–69.

24   Juan J. Walte, "Greenpeace: 200,000 Died in Gulf," *USA Today,* May 30, 1991, p. 1A.

25   Kim Cobb, "Vets Warn of Risks to Soldiers' Health: Critics Fear Repeat of Gulf War Illnesses," *Houston Chronicle,* February 9, 2003, p. 1.

26   James Meikle, " 'Health Will Suffer for Years,' " *The Guardian* (London), November 12, 2003, p. 17.

27   Joel Brinkley, "American Companies Rebuilding Iraq Find They Are Having to Start from the Ground Up," *New York Times,* February 22, 2004, p. 1: 11. Tucker Carlson, "Hired Guns," *Esquire,* March 2004, pp. 130–38.

28   Felicity Barringer, "Security Council Votes to Revive Oil-for-Food Program in Iraq," *New York Times,* March 29, 2003, p. B7.

Notes

29   Dan Morgan and Karen DeYoung, "Hill Panels Approve War Funds, With Curbs: Most Restrictions Aimed at Pentagon," *Washington Post,* April 2, 2003, p. A26.

30   Lou Dobbs, *Lou Dobb's Moneyline,* CNN, March 27, 2003.

31   Greg Wright, "French Fries? Mais Non, Congress Calls Em Freedom Fries," Gannett News Service, March 12, 2003, http://www.gannettonline.com/gns/faceoff2/20030312-18 100.shtml.

32   Serge Bellanger, "Of Wal-Marts, BMWs and Brie," *Chicago Tribune,* April 27, 2003, p. 9.

33   George W. Bush, Camp David, Maryland, press briefing, September 16, 2001: "[W]e're going to do it. We will rid the world of the evildoers. We will call together freedom-loving people to fight terrorism. And so on this day of—on the Lord's day, I say to my fellow Americans, thank you for your prayers, thank you for your compassion, thank you for your love for one another and tomorrow when you get back to work, work hard like you always have. But we've been warned. We've been warned there are evil people in this world. We've been warned so vividly and we'll be alert. Your government is alert. The governors and mayors are alert that evil folks still lurk out there."

CHAPTER 3: INSTANT-MIX IMPERIAL DEMOCRACY

1   Molly Moore, "The USS Vincennes and a Deadly Mistake: Highly Sophisticated Combat Ship at Center of Defense Department Investigation," *Washington Post,* July 4, 1988, p. A23.

2   R.W. Apple, Jr., "Bush Appears in Trouble Despite Two Big Advantages," *New York Times,* August 4, 1988, p. A1. See Lewis Lapham, *Theater of War* (New York: New Press, 2002), p. 126.

3   Patrick E. Tyler and Janet Elder, "Threats and Responses: The Poll: Poll Finds Most In U.S. Support Delaying a War," *New York Times,* February 14, 2003, p. A1.

4   Maureen Dowd, "The Xanax Cowboy," *New York Times,* March 9, 2003, p. 4: 13.

5   President George W. Bush, address to the nation, State Floor Cross Hallway, the White House, Federal News Service, March 17, 2003, http://www.whitehouse.gov/news/releases/2003/03/20030319-17.html.

6   President George W. Bush, speech at the Cincinnati Museum Center, Cincinnati, Ohio, Federal News Service, October 7, 2002, http://www.whitehouse.gov/news/releases/2002/10/20021007-8.html.

7   See Saïd K. Aburish, *Saddam Hussein: The Politics of Revenge* (London: Bloomsbury, 2001). See also the PBS *Frontline* interview with Aburish, "Secrets of His Life and Leadership," from *The Survival of Saddam,* http://www.pbs.org/wgbh/pages/frontline/shows/saddam/interviews/aburish.html.

8   See Anthony Arnove, "Indonesia: Crisis and Revolt," *International Socialist Review* 5 (Fall 1998).

9   Originally stated in a May 1980 interview on the *MacNeil/Lehrer Report* on PBS. Quoted in Philip Geyelin, "Forget Gunboat Diplomacy," *Washington Post,* September 29, 1980, p. A13.

10 See Anthony Arnove, ed., *Iraq Under Siege: The Deadly Impact of Sanctions and War,* 2nd ed. (Cambridge, MA: South End Press, 2002), especially the chapter by Noam Chomsky, "US Iraq Policy: Consequences and Motives," pp. 65–74, and Arnove's Introduction, pp. 11–31.

11 See, among many other of Bush's speeches, his address to the Wings over the Rockies Air and Space Museum, Denver, Colorado, Federal News Service, October 28, 2002, in which he reminded his audience that Hussein "is a person who has gassed his own people.... [H]e's anxious to have, once again to develop a nuclear weapon. He's got connections with al Qaeda." Bush also commented: "We love life, everybody matters as far as we're concerned, everybody is precious. They have no regard for innocent life whatsoever. (Applause.) They hate the fact that we love freedom. We love our freedom of religion, we love our freedom of speech, we love every aspect of freedom. (Applause.) And we're not changing. (Applause.) We're not intimidated. As a matter of fact, the more they hate our freedoms, the more we love our freedoms. (Applause.)" http://www.whitehouse.gov/news/releases/2002/10/2002 1028-5.html

12 See Arnove, *Iraq Under Siege,* pp. 68–69.

13 "We are a nation called to defend freedom—a freedom that is not the grant of any government or document, but is our endowment from God." See Dan Eggen, "Ashcroft Invokes Religion in U.S. War on Terrorism," *Washington Post,* February 20, 2002, p. A2.

14 Michael R. Gordon, "Baghdad's Power Vacuum Is Drawing Only Dissent," *New York Times,* April 21, 2003, p. A10.

15 Peter Beaumont, "Anger Rises as US Fails to Control Anarchy," *The Observer* (London), April 13, 2003, p. 3.

16 Jim Dwyer, "Troops Endure Blowing Sands and Mud Rain," *New York Times,* March 26, 2003, p. A1; Neela Banerjee, "Army Depots in Iraqi Desert Have Names of Oil Giants," *New York Times,* March 27, 2003, p. C14.

17 Secretary of Defense Donald H. Rumsfeld, Defense Department operational update briefing, Pentagon Briefing Room, Arlington, Virginia, Federal News Service, April 11, 2003.

18 Reuters, "Number Imprisoned Exceeds 2 Million, Justice Dept. Says," *Washington Post,* April 7, 2003, p. A4; The Sentencing Project, "U.S. Prison Populations: Trends and Implications," May 2003, p. 1, http://www.sentencingproject. org/pdfs/1044.pdf.

Arundhati Roy

19 The Sentencing Project, "U.S. Prison Populations," p 1.

20 Fox Butterfield, "Prison Rates among Blacks Reach a Peak, Report Finds," *New York Times,* April 7, 2003, p. A12.

21 Richard Willing, "More Seeking President's Pardon," *USA Today,* December 24, 2002, p. 3A.

22 Paul Martin, Ed Vulliamy, and Gaby Hinsliff, "US Army Was Told to Protect Looted Museum," *The Observer* (London), April 20, 2003, p. 4; Frank Rich, "And Now: 'Operation Iraqi Looting'," *New York Times,* April 27, 2003, p. 2: 1.

23 See Scott Peterson, "Iraq: Saladin to Saddam," *Christian Science Monitor,* March 4, 2003, p. 1.

24 Secretary of Defense Donald H. Rumsfeld, Defense Department operational update briefing, Pentagon Briefing Room, Arlington, Virginia, Federal News Service, April 11, 2003.

25 Martin, Vulliamy, and Hinsliff, "US Army Was Told to Protect Looted Museum," p. 4.

26 See Robert Fisk, "Americans Defend Two Untouchable Ministries from the Hordes of Looters," *The Independent* (London), April 14, 2003, p. 7:

> "Iraq's scavengers have thieved and destroyed what they have been allowed to loot and burn by the Americans—and a two-hour drive around Baghdad shows clearly what the US intends to protect. After days of arson and pillage, here's a short but revealing scorecard. US troops have sat back and allowed mobs to wreck and then burn the Ministry of Planning, the Ministry of Education, the Ministry of Irrigation, the Ministry of Trade, the Ministry of Industry, the Ministry of Foreign Affairs, the Ministry of Culture and the Ministry of Information. They did nothing to prevent looters from destroying priceless treasures of Iraq's history in the Baghdad Archaeological Museum and in the museum in the northern city of Mosul, or from looting three hospitals.

Notes

"The Americans have, though, put hundreds of troops inside two Iraqi ministries that remain untouched—and untouchable—because tanks and armoured personnel carriers and Humvees have been placed inside and outside both institutions. And which ministries proved to be so important for the Americans? Why, the Ministry of Interior, of course—with its vast wealth of intelligence information on Iraq—and the Ministry of Oil."

27   Carlotta Gall, "In Afghanistan, Violence Stalls Renewal Effort," *New York Times,* April 26, 2003, p. A1. See also David Rohde, "U.S. Rebuked on Afghans in Detention," *New York Times,* March 8, 2004, p. A6.

28   Scott Lindlaw, "Accommodating TV-Friendly Presidential Visit Caused a Few Changes in Navy Carrier's Routine," Associated Press, May 2, 2003.

29   Walter V. Robinson, "1-Year Gap in Bush's Guard Duty: No Record of Airman at Drills in 1972–73," *Boston Globe,* May 23, 2000, p. A1.

30   David E. Sanger, "Bush Declares 'One Victory in a War on Terror,'" *New York Times,* May 2, 2003, p. A1.

31   James Harding, "Bush to Hail Triumph but Not Declare a US Victory," *Financial Times* (London), May 1, 2003, p. 8.

32   Quoted in John R. MacArthur, "In the Psychological Struggle, Nations Wield Their Weapons of Mass Persuasion," *Boston Globe,* March 9, 2003, p. D12.

33   General Tommy Franks, *Sunday Morning,* CBS, March 23, 2003.

34   " 'Non' Campaigner Chirac Ready to Address French," *Daily Mail* (London), March 20, 2003, p. 13.

35   Robert J. McCartney, "Germany Stops Short of Saying 'I Told You So': Opposition to War Vindicated, Officials Say," *Washington Post,* April 3, 2003, p. A33: "Although Germany formally opposes the war, it is supporting the U.S. effort through such steps as overflight rights and special security at

U.S. bases in Germany. Officials say Germany is doing more for the war than any country except Britain." See also Giles Tremlett and John Hooper, "War in the Gulf: Clampdown on Coverage of Returning Coffins," *The Guardian* (London), March 27, 2003, p. 3.

36 Judy Dempsey and Robert Graham, "Paris Gives First Signs of Support to Coalition," *Financial Times* (London), April 4, 2003, p. 4.

37 Interfax, "Putin Wants US Victory," *Hobart Mercury* (Australia), April 4, 2003.

38 Morton Abramowitz, "Turkey and Iraq, Act II," *Wall Street Journal,* January 16, 2003, p. A12.

39 Noam Chomsky, *Hegemony or Survival: America's Quest for Global Dominance* (New York: Metropolitan Books, 2004), p. 131.

40 Angelique Chrisafis et al., "Millions Worldwide Rally for Peace," *The Guardian* (London), February 17, 2003, p. 6, http://www.guardian.co.uk/antiwar/story/0,12809,897098, 00.html.

41 Richard W. Stevenson, "Antiwar Protests Fail to Sway Bush on Plans for Iraq," *New York Times,* February 19, 2003, p. A1.

42 David McDonald and John Pape, "South Africa: Cost Recovery Is Not Sustainable," Africa News, August 30, 2002; David McDonald and John Pape, eds., *Cost Recovery and the Crisis of Service Delivery in South Africa* (London: Zed Press, 2002). See also Ashwin Desai, *We Are the Poors: Community Struggles in Post-Apartheid South Africa* (New York: Monthly Review Press, 2002).

43 "Africa's Engine," *The Economist,* January 17, 2004.

44 Paul Betts, "Ciampi Calls for Review of Media Laws," *Financial Times* (London), July 24, 2002, p. 8. For an overview of Berlusconi's holdings, see Ketupa.net Media Profiles: http://www.ketupa.net/berlusconi1.htm.

45 Frank Bruni, "Berlusconi, in a Rough Week, Says Only He Can Save Italy," *New York Times,* May 10, 2003, p. A1.

Notes

46   Tim Burt, "Mays on a Charm Offensive: The Clear Channel Chief Is Seeking to Answer His Group's Critics," *Financial Times* (London), October 27, 2003, p. 27. See also John Dunbar and Aron Pilhofer, "Big Radio Rules in Small Markets," The Center for Public Integrity, October 1, 2003, http://www.publicintegrity.org/telecom/report.aspx?aid=63&sid=200.

47   Douglas Jehl, "Across Country, Thousands Gather to Back U.S. Troops and Policy," *New York Times,* March 24, 2003, p. B15.

48   Frank Rich, "Iraq Around The Clock," *New York Times,* March 30, 2003, p. 2: 1.

49   Bagdikian, *The New Media Monopoly.*

50   Tom Shales, "Michael Powell and the FCC: Giving Away the Marketplace of Ideas," *Washington Post,* June 2, 2003, p. C1; Paul Davidson and David Lieberman, "FCC Eases Rules for Media Mergers," *USA Today,* June 3, 2003, p. 1A.

51   David Leonhardt, "Bush's Record on Jobs: Risking Comparison to a Republican Ghost," *New York Times,* July 3, 2003, p. C1.

52   Robert Tanner, "Report Says State Budget Gaps Jumped by Nearly 50 Percent, with Next Year Looking Worse," Associated Press, February 5, 2003.

53   Dana Milbank and Mike Allen, "Bush to Ask Congress for $80 Billion: Estimate of War's Cost Comes as Thousands March in Protest," *Washington Post,* March 23, 2003, p. A1.

54   Sheryl Gay Stolberg, "Senators' Sons in War: An Army of One," *New York Times,* March 22, 2003, p. B10. See also David M. Halbfinger and Steven A. Holmes, "Military Mirrors a Working-Class America," *New York Times,* March 30, 2003, p. A1.

55   Darryl Fears, "Draft Bill Stirs Debate Over The Military, Race and Equity," *Washington Post,* February 4, 2003, p. A3.

56 David Cole, "Denying Felons Vote Hurts Them, Society," *USA Today,* February 3, 2000, p. 17A; "From Prison to the Polls," editorial, *Christian Science Monitor,* May 24, 2001, p. 10.

57 See Cole, "Denying Felons" and sidebar: "Not at the Ballot Box."

58 Kenneth J. Cooper, "In India's Kerala, Quality of Life Is High but Opportunity Is Limited," *Washington Post,* January 3, 1997, p. A35; Amartya Sen, *Development As Freedom* (New York: Alfred A. Knopf, 1999). See also Fareed Zakaria, "Beyond Money," *New York Times Book Review,* November 28, 1999, p. 14.

59 Linda Villarosa, "As Black Men Move Into Middle Age, Dangers Rise," *New York Times,* September 23, 2002, p. F1.

60 Amy Goldstein and Dana Milbank, "Bush Joins Admissions Case Fight: U-Mich. Use of Race Is Called 'Divisive,'" *Washington Post,* January 16, 2003, p. A1; James Harding, "Bush Scrambles to Bolster Civil Rights Credibility," *Financial Times* (London), January 21, 2003, p. 10.

61 Elizabeth Becker and Richard A. Oppel, Jr., "Bechtel Top Contender In Bidding Over Iraq," *New York Times,* March 29, 2003, p. B6.

62 André Verlöy and Daniel Politi, with Aron Pilhofer, "Advisors of Influence: Nine Members of the Defense Policy Board Have Ties to Defense Contractors," Center for Public Integrity, March 28, 2003, http://www.publicintegrity. org/report.aspx?aid=91&sid=200.

63 Laura Peterson, "Bechtel Group Inc.," Center for Public Integrity, http://www.publicintegrity.org/wow/bio.aspx?act =pro&ddlC=6.

64 Peterson, "Bechtel Group Inc."

65 Bob Herbert, "Spoils of War," *New York Times,* April 10, 2003, p. A27.

66 Quoted in Herbert, "Spoils of War."

Notes

67 Karen DeYoung and Jackie Spinner, "Contract for Rebuilding of Iraq Awarded to Bechtel: U.S. Firm 1 of 6 Invited to Bid for $680 Million Project," *Washington Post,* April 18, 2003, p. A23. In December 2003, the contract was raised by $350 million, to $1.03 billion. In January 2004, Bechtel won a contract worth another $1.8 billion. See Elizabeth Douglass and John Hendren, "Bechtel Wins Another Iraq Deal," *Los Angeles Times,* January 7, 2004, p. C2.

68 Stephen J. Glain, "Bechtel Wins Pact to Help Rebuild Iraq: Closed-Bid Deal Could Total $680M," *Boston Globe,* April 18, 2003, p. A1.

69 Robin Toner and Neil A. Lewis, "House Passes Terrorism Bill Much Like Senate's, but with 5-Year Limit," *New York Times,* October 13, 2001, p. B6.

70 See Cole, *Enemy Aliens,* pp. 57–69.

71 Evelyn Nieves, "Local Officials Rise Up to Defy the Patriot Act," *Washington Post,* April 21, 2003, p. A1.

72 See Cole, *Enemy Aliens.*

73 Amnesty International, "India: Abuse of the Law in Gujarat: Muslims Detained Illegally in Ahmedabad," November 6, 2003, AI index no. ASA 20/029/2003, http://web.amnesty. org/library/Index/ENGASA200292003?open&of=ENG-I ND. See also "People's Tribunal Highlights Misuse of POTA," *The Hindu,* March 18, 2004; and Sanghamitra Chakraborty et al., "Slaves in Draconia: Ordinary Folks—Minors, Farmers, Minorities—Fall Prey to POTA for No Fault of Theirs," *Outlook India,* March 22, 2004.

74 Greg Myre, "Shootout in West Bank Kills an Israeli Soldier and a Palestinian," *New York Times,* March 13, 2003, p. A5.

75 Wayne Washington, "More Opposition to Detentions in Terror Probe," *Boston Globe,* May 13, 2002, p. A1; Tamar Lewin, "As Authorities Keep Up Immigration Arrests, Detainees Ask Why They Are Targets," *New York Times,* February 3, 2002, p. 1: 14.

76 Neil King, Jr., "Bush Officials Draft Broad Plan For Free-Market Economy in Iraq," *Wall Street Journal,* May 1, 2003, p. A1.

77 Naomi Klein, "Iraq Is Not America's to Sell," *The Guardian* (London), November 7, 2003, p. 27. See also Jeff Madrick, "The Economic Plan for Iraq Seems Long on Ideology, Short on Common Sense," *New York Times,* October 2, 2003, p. C2.

78 David Usborne, "US Firm Is Hired to Purge Schools of Saddam's Doctrine," *The Independent* (London), April 22, 2003, p. 10; Steve Johnson, "Scramble to Win the Spoils of War," *Financial Times* (London) April 23, 2003, p. 27; Paul Richter and Edmund Sanders, "Contracts Go to Allies of Iraq's Chalabi," *Los Angeles Times,* November 7, 2003, p. A1.

79 Heather Stewart, "Iraq: After the War: Fury at Agriculture Post for US Grain Dealer," *The Guardian* (London), April 28, 2003, p. 11.

80 Alan Cowell, "British Ask What a War Would Mean for Business," *New York Times,* March 18, 2003, p. W1; "Spoils of War," editorial, *San Francisco Chronicle,* March 29, 2003, p. A14; Jan Hennop, "S. African Apartheid Victims File Lawsuit in US Court, Name Companies," Agence France-Presse, November 12, 2002; Nicol Degli Innocenti, "African Workers Launch Dollars 100bn Lawsuit," *Financial Times* (London), October 13, 2003, p. 9.

81 John Vidal, "Shell Fights Fires as Strife Flares in Delta," *The Guardian* (London), September 15, 1999, p. 15; Vidal, "Oil Wealth Buys Health in Country Within a Country," *The Guardian* (London), September 16, 1999, p. 19. See also Ike Okonta and Oronto Douglas, *Where Vultures Feast: Shell, Human Rights, and Oil* (New York: Verso, 2003) and Al Gedicks, *Resource Rebels: Native Challenges to Mining and Oil Corporations* (Cambridge, MA: South End Press, 2001).

82 Tom Brokaw, speaking to Vice Admiral Dennis McGinn, *NBC News Special Report: Target Iraq,* NBC, March 19, 2003.

Notes

83 Bryan Bender, "Roadblocks Seen in Sept. 11 Inquiry," *Boston Globe,* July 9, 2003, p. A2. See also Josh Meyer, "Terror Not a Bush Priority Before 9/11, Witness Says," *Los Angeles Times,* March 25, 2004, p. A1, and Edward Alden, "Tale of Intelligence Failure Above and Below," *Financial Times* (London), March 26, 2004, p. 2.

84 Howard Zinn, *A People's History of the United States,* 20th anniversary ed. (New York: HarperCollins, 2000). See also Anthony Arnove and Howard Zinn, *Voices of a People's History of the United States* (New York: Seven Stories Press, 2004).

CHAPTER 4: WHEN THE SAINTS GO MARCHING OUT

1 See Arundhati Roy, "Democracy: Who Is She When She Is at Home?" in *War Talk,* pp. 17–44.

2 "Cong[ress Party] Ploy Fails, Modi Steals the Show in Pain," *Indian Express,* August 16, 2003.

3 Agence France-Presse, "Indian Activists Urge Mandela to Snub Gujarat Government Invite," August 4, 2003; "Guj[arat]–Mandela," The Press Trust of India, August 5, 2003; "Battle for Gujarat's Image Now on Foreign Soil," *The Times of India,* August 7, 2003.

4 Agence France-Presse, "'Relax, Mandela Isn't Coming, He's Working on a Book," August 5, 2003.

5 Michael Dynes, "Mbeki Can Seize White Farms under New Law," *The Times* (London), January 31, 2004, p. 26.

6 Dynes, "Mbeki Can Seize White Farms."

7 Patrick Laurence, "South Africa Fights to Put the Past to Rest," *The Irish Times,* December 28, 2000, p. 57.

8 Anthony Stoppard, "South Africa: Water, Electricity Cutoffs Affect 10 Million," Inter Press Service, March 21, 2002.

9 Henri E. Cauvin, "Hunger in Southern Africa Imperils Lives of Millions," *New York Times,* April 26, 2002, p. A8; James Lamont, "Nobody Says 'No' to Mandela," *Financial Times*

(London), December 10, 2002, p. 4; Patrick Laurence, "South Africans Sceptical of Official Data," *The Irish Times,* June 6, 2003, p. 30.

10 See Desai, *We Are The Poors.*

11 South African Press Association, "Gauteng Municipalities to Target Service Defaulters," May 4, 1999; Alison Maitland, "Combining to Harness the Power of Private Enterprise," *Financial Times* (London), August 23, 2002, Survey: "Sustainable Business," p. 2.

12 Nicol Degli Innocenti and John Reed, "SA Govt Opposes Reparations Lawsuit," *Financial Times* (London), May 19, 2003, p. 15.

13 South African Press Association, "SAfrica Asks US Court to Dismiss Apartheid Reparations Cases," BBC Worldwide Monitoring, July 30, 2003.

14 Martin Luther King, Jr., *A Testament of Hope: The Essential Writings and Speeches of Martin Luther King, Jr.,* ed. James M. Washington (New York: HarperCollins, 1991), p. 233.

15 King, *A Testament of Hope,* p. 233.

16 "Men of Vietnam," *New York Times,* April 9, 1967, Week in Review, p. 2E. Quoted in Mike Marqusee, *Redemption Song: Muhammad Ali and the Spirit of the Sixties* (New York: Verso, 1999), p. 217.

17 King, *A Testament of Hope,* p. 245.

18 Halbfinger and Holmes, "Military Mirrors a Working-Class America"; Fears, "Draft Bill Stirs Debate Over The Military, Race and Equity."

19 Cole, "Denying Felons" and sidebar; "From Prison to the Polls," editorial, *Christian Science Monitor.*

20 King, *A Testament of Hope,* p. 239.

21 Quoted in Marqusee, *Redemption Song,* p. 218.

22 King, *A Testament of Hope,* p. 250.

23 Marqusee, *Redemption Song,* pp. 1–4, 292.

Notes

CHAPTER 5: IN MEMORY OF SHANKAR GUHA NIYOGI

1   Human Rights Watch, "India: Human Rights Developments," *Human Rights Watch World Report 1993*, http://www.hrw.org/reports/1993/WR93/Asw-06.htm.

CHAPTER 6: DO TURKEYS ENJOY THANKSGIVING?

1   See the website of The Project for The New American Century: http://www.newamericancentury.org. See also Verlöy and Politi, with Pilhofer, "Advisors of Influence."

2   "Strike Not Your Right Anymore: SC [Supreme Court] to Govt Staff," *Indian Express*, August 7, 2003; "Trade Unions Protest Against SC [Supreme Court] Order on Strikes," *The Times of India*, August 8, 2003.

3   See Arundhati Roy, "On Citizens' Rights to Dissent," in *War Talk*, pp. 87–104.

4   Michael Jensen, "Denis Halliday: Iraq Sanctions Are Genocide," *The Daily Star*, Lebanon, July 7, 2000. See also the interview with Halliday and Phyllis Bennis in Arnove, *Iraq Under Siege*, pp. 53–64.

5   Arnove, *Iraq Under Siege*, pp. 103–04.

6   Joseph E. Stiglitz, *Globalization and Its Discontents* (New York: W.W. Norton, 2002), pp. 7, 61, 253–54.

7   "World Trade Special Report," *The Independent* (London), September 10, 2003, p. 1; Thompson Ayodele, "Last Chance for Fair Go on Trade," *Australian Financial Review*, September 11, 2003, p. B63.

8   George Monbiot, *The Age of Consent* (New York: The New Press, 2004), p. 158. See also U.N. General Assembly, *External Debt Crisis and Development: Report to the Secretary-General*, A/57/253, 2003, p. 2, http://www.un.dk/doc/A570253.pdf.

9   The Fifth WTO Ministerial Conference was held in Cancún, Mexico, from September 10 to 14, 2003. Sue Kirchhoff and

James Cox, "WTO Talks Break Down, Threatening Future Pact," *USA Today,* September 15, 2003, p. 1B.

CHAPTER 7: HOW DEEP SHALL WE DIG?

1   Hina Kausar Alam and P. Balu, "J&K [Jammu and Kashmir] Fudges DNA Samples to Cover Up Killings," *Times of India,* March 7, 2002.

2   See Roy, "Democracy: Who Is She When She Is at Home?"

3   Somit Sen, "Shooting Turns Spotlight on Encounter Cops," *Times of India,* August 23, 2003.

4   W. Chandrakanth, "Crackdown on Civil Liberties Activists in the Offing?" *The Hindu,* October 4, 2003: "...several activists have gone underground fearing police reprisals. Their fears are not unfounded, as the State police have been staging encounters at will. While the police frequently release the statistics on naxalite violence, they avoid mentioning the victims of their own violence. The Andhra Pradesh Civil Liberties Committee (APCLC), which is keeping track of the police killings, has listed more than 4,000 deaths, 2,000 of them in the last eight years alone." See also K.T. Sangameswaran, "Rights Activists Allege Ganglord—Cop Nexus," *The Hindu,* October 22, 2003.

5   David Rohde, "India and Kashmir Separatists Begin Talks on Ending Strife," *New York Times,* January 23, 2004, p. A8; Deutsche Presse-Agentur, "Thousands Missing, Unmarked Graves Tell Kashmir Story," October 7, 2003.

6   Unpublished reports from the Association of Parents of Disappeared People (APDP), Srinagar.

7   See also Edward Luce, "Kashmir's New Leader Promises 'Healing Touch,'" *Financial Times* (London), October 28, 2002, p. 12.

Notes

8 Ray Marcelo, "Anti-Terrorism Law Backed by India's Supreme Court," *Financial Times* (London), December 17, 2003, p. 2.

9 People's Union for Civil Liberties (PUCL), "A Preliminary Fact Finding on POTA Cases in Jharkhand," Delhi, India, May 2, 2003, http://www.pucl.org/Topics/Law/2003/poto-jharkhand.htm.

10 "People's Tribunal Highlights Misuse of POTA," *The Hindu,* March 18, 2004.

11 "People's Tribunal." See also "Human Rights Watch Ask Centre to Repeal POTA," The Press Trust of India, September 8, 2002.

12 Leena Misra, "240 POTA Cases, All against Minorities," *Times of India,* September 15, 2003; "People's Tribunal Highlights Misuse of POTA," March 18, 2004. The *Times of India* misreported the testimony presented. As the Press Trust of India article notes, in Gujarat, "The only non-Muslim in the list is a Sikh, Liversingh Tej Singh Sikligar, who figured in it for an attempt on the life of Surat lawyer Hasmukh Lalwala, and allegedly hung himself in a police lock-up in Surat in April [2003]." On Gujarat, see Roy, "Democracy: Who Is She When She Is at Home?"

13 "A Pro-Police Report," *The Hindu,* March 20, 2004; Amnesty International, "India: Report of the Malimath Committee on Reforms of the Criminal Justice System: Some Comments," September 19, 2003 (ASA 20/025/2003).

14 "J&K [Jammu and Kashmir] Panel Wants Draconian Laws Withdrawn," *The Hindu,* March 23, 2003. See also South Asian Human Rights Documentation Center (SAHRDC), "Armed Forces Special Powers Act: A Study in National Security Tyranny," November 1995, http://www.nscnonline.org/webpage/Articles/south_asia_human_rights1.htm.

15 See "Growth of a Demon: Genesis of the Armed Forces (Special Powers) Act, 1958" and related documents, in

Manipur Update, December 1999, http://www.geocities.com/manipurupdate/december_feature_1.htm.

16 On the lack of any convictions for the massacres in Gujarat, see Edward Luce, "Master of Ambiguity," *Financial Times* (London), April 3–4, 2004, p. 16. On the March 31, 1997, murder of Chandrashekhar Prasad, see Andrew Nash, "An Election at JNU," *Himal,* December 2003, http://www.himalmag.com/2003/december/perspective.htm. For more information on the additional crimes listed here, see pp. 87–90 above.

17 N.A. Mujumdar, "Eliminate Hunger Now, Poverty Later," *Business Line,* January 8, 2003.

18 "Foodgrain Exports May Slow Down This Fiscal [Year]," *India Business Insight,* June 2, 2003; "India: Agriculture Sector: Paradox of Plenty," *Business Line,* June 26, 2001; Ranjit Devraj, "Farmers Protest against Globalization," Inter Press Service, January 25, 2001.

19 Utsa Patnaik, "Falling Per Capita Availability of Foodgrains for Human Consumption in the Reform Period in India," *Akhbar* 2 (October 2001), http://66.51.111.239/indowindow/threeessays/contact.php; P. Sainath, "Have Tornado, Will Travel," *The Hindu Magazine,* August 18, 2002; Sylvia Nasar, "Profile: The Conscience of the Dismal Science," *New York Times,* January 9, 1994, p. 3: 8. Maria Misra, "Heart of Smugness: Unlike Belgium, Britain Is Still Complacently Ignoring the Gory Cruelties of Its Empire," *The Guardian* (London), July 23, 2002, p. 15. See also Utsa Patnaik, "On Measuring 'Famine' Deaths: Different Criteria for Socialism and Capitalism?" *Akhbar* 6 (November–December 1999), http://www.indowindow.com/akhbar/article.php?article=74&category=8&issue=9.

20 Amartya Sen, *Development As Freedom.*

21 "The Wasted India," *The Statesman* (India), February 17, 2001. "Child-Blain," *The Statesman* (India), November 24, 2001.

Notes

22 Utsa Patnaik, "The Republic of Hunger," lecture, Jawaharlal Nehru University, New Delhi, India, April 10, 2004, http://macroscan.com/fet/apr04/fet210404Republic_Hunger. htm.

23 Praful Bidwai, "India amidst Serious Agrarian Crisis," *Central Chronicle* (Bhopal), April 9, 2004.

24 Roy, *Power Politics,* 2nd ed., p. 13.

25 See Mike Davis, *Late Victorian Holocausts: El Niño Famines and the Making of the Third World* (New York: Verso, 2002).

26 Among other sources, see Edwin Black, *IBM and the Holocaust: The Strategic Alliance Between Nazi Germany and America's Most Powerful Corporation* (New York: Three Rivers Press, 2003).

27 "For India Inc., Silence Protects the Bottom Line," *The Times of India,* February 17, 2003. "CII Apologises to Modi," *The Hindu,* March 7, 2003.

28 India was the only country to abstain on December 22, 2003, from U.N. General Assembly Resolution, "Protection of Human Rights and Fundamental Freedoms While Countering Terrorism," A/RES/58/187. Quoted in Amnesty International India, "Security Legislation and State Accountability: A Presentation for the POTA People's Hearing, March 13–14, New Delhi," http://www.un.org/ Depts/dhl/resguide/r58.htm.

INDEX

Index

FBI (Federal Bureau of
  Investigation), 62
Federal Communications
  Commission (US), 58–59
Financial Times, 57
Fischer, Joschka, 53
Fluor, 64
France, 27, 33, 52–53
Franks, Tommy, 52, 58
freedom: Bush on, 129n33 (38),
  130n11 (46); elites and, 70,
  103–4; in India, 81; Iraq War
  and, 35; loss of, 17, 41, 58, 63,
  103–4; sources of, 66–67, 116;
  US and, 47, 49, 58, 63, 131n13
free market, 2, 3, 55, 86, 105. *See
  also* economics

G

Gallup International, 53
Gandhi, Mohandas K., 70, 71, 91
Geneva Convention, 27–28, 51
genocide: by Saddam Hussein,
  45–46, 76, 89, 130n11; in India,
  106–7; against Iraq, 31, 35,
  88–89; against Muslims, 7–8,
  70–71, 85, 99–101, 106, 108;
  against Sikhs, 8, 96, 101; by US,
  74. *See also* violence
Germany, 33, 52–53, 133n35
globalization: democracy subverted
  by, 3–4, 20, 55, 86, 89–91,
  104–5; in India, 12, 20, 104–5,
  109–10; in Iraq, 80–81;
  opposition to, 34, 88, 90;
  poverty and, 12, 86, 88, 110; US
  and, 34, 61–62
Godhra train attack, 96–97

Goering, Hermann, 52
Great Britain: attitudes toward, 34,
  36–37; Hussein's Iraq supported
  by, 45–46; imperialism in India,
  81, 91, 108, 117; in Iraq war,
  23–30, 37, 48, 53–54, 133n35;
  media in, 27–29, 37; trade by,
  89. *See also* Blair, Tony
Guantánamo Bay, Cuba, 27–28
Gujarat: genocide in, 7–8, 70–71,
  85, 99, 101, 106, 108; Muslims
  in, 12; police violence, 10, 110;
  resistance movements in, 14;
  terrorism in, 98–99, 143n12
Gulf War (1991), 18, 31, 46, 76
Guttmann, Nick, 30

H

Halabja, Iraq, 46
Halliburton, 33, 86
Halliday, Denis, 88
Hamer, Fannie Lou, 77
Hammurabi Code, 49–50
Hindus: fundamentalist, 8, 15,
  96–97, 110, 114–15; and
  Muslims, 7–8, 70–71, 80, 85,
  96–101, 106–9; nationalism and,
  71, 80, 97, 109–10, 112–13, 116;
  social services provided by, 110,
  114–15
Hindutva, 71, 105–6, 113
Hoon, Geoff, 26
humanitarian aid, 30, 32, 35, 88–89
human rights, 8–9, 12, 14, 103–4,
  111, 115. *See also* civil rights
Hungary, 53–54
Hussein, Saddam: fall of, 29, 48, 53,
  85–86, 93; Iran and, 76; Iraq war

Index

and, 23–24, 26, 46; repression and genocide by, 31, 45–46, 76, 89, 130n11; terrorism and, 24, 43–44, 130n11; US and, 18, 38, 44, 76

I

imperialism: British, 91, 108, 117; colonialism and, 55, 70, 89, 92, 108; democracy and, 56; economic, 53, 84–85; media and, 83–85; military, 46–47, 84–86; opposition to, 42, 66, 70, 82, 93–94; racism and, 47, 55, 87; revival of, 83–84, 87; US, 34, 39, 42–47, 53, 66–67, 83–84, 94

Independent on Sunday (UK), 30

India: corporate influence in, 20, 87, 104–5, 109–10; democracy and, 20, 55, 100–101; economy of, 79, 81, 86–87, 101–5, 108–10; fascism in, 108–9; imperialism in, 81–82, 91, 108; international affairs, 94; law and courts, 9, 14–17, 81, 86, 98–100, 111; media in, 1–3, 101; military, 2, 94, 100–101; religious nationalism in, 71, 80, 96–97, 101, 107–13, 116; repression in, 3, 11, 98–101; resistance movements, 8–12, 70, 79–82, 101, 103–4, 111–18; violence in, 2–3, 8–12, 81, 94–97, 101, 107–11

Indian Express, 15

India Today, 15

infrastructure: in India, 13–14, 20, 87, 104–5, 109; in Iraq, 25,

48–50, 64, 76–77, 80–81; in poor countries, 84. *See also* dams

International Monetary Fund (IMF), 34, 69, 88, 90

Internet, 3, 34

Iran, 42, 46, 76

Iraq: corporate influence over, 61–62, 64, 77, 80–81, 137n67; economy, 25, 29–33, 50–51, 62–64, 76, 80–81; invasion and occupation of, 5, 76–77, 80–81, 84, 93–94, 97; law in, 46, 49–50, 63–64; media coverage of, 26–30, 33; military and weapons, 5, 25–26, 29, 34–35, 43–46, 76; Muslims in, 29, 45; oil, 32, 53, 64, 132n26; politics, 29, 45–46, 80–81; repression and genocide in, 31, 43–46, 76, 88–89, 130n11; sanctions against, 25, 31, 76, 89; society and culture, 18, 49–50, 132n26; terrorism and, 24, 43; UN and, 25, 32, 76, 94; violence and looting in, 48, 50, 132n26; weapons of mass destruction, 34–35, 44. *See also* Hussein, Saddam; Iraq war

Iraq war (2003): economic aspects, 30, 48, 50, 59; effects, 29–30, 32–34, 48–51, 59, 126n3; legal issues, 27, 53–54; media coverage, 23–24, 29–30, 33, 43, 50; military and strategic aspects, 5, 23–30, 34–35, 43–44, 48, 51–54, 133n35; opposition to, 37, 52–54, 76, 92; preparations, 5, 43–45; prisoners, 27; racism of, 36, 76–77

ISI (Inter Services
Intelligence—Pakistan), 11, 97
Israel, 86
Italy, 53–54, 57

J

Jammu and Kashmir state, 12,
100–101
Jharkhand, 10, 12–13, 98, 110, 111
Joint Inquiry into Intelligence
Community Activities (US), 65

K

Kargil war, 2, 100. *See also* Kashmir
Kashmir, 2–3, 12–13, 85, 95–98,
100–101, 111–12
Kennedy, John F., 45
Kerala, 10–12, 18–19, 60, 110
Khan, I.G., 95n
King, Martin Luther, Jr., 60, 69,
73–75, 77
King, Rodney, 49
Koel Karo dam, 10
Kurdish people, 46, 76

L

labor, 13, 64, 79–81, 86
Lalwala, Hasmukh, 143n12
law: economics and, 9, 14–15, 73,
81, 86; globalization and, 55, 86,
89; history, 49–50; in India, 8–9,
14–17, 86, 98–100, 111; politics
and, 16, 56–57, 59, 111; POTA,
12, 98–100, 103, 111, 113;
resistance movements and,
62–63, 91; terrorism and, 62,
98–100, 103; in US, 59, 73

Lenin, V.I., 64
life expectancy, 60
Linlithgow, Lord, 101
Lula da Silva, Luiz Inácio, 90

M

Madhya Pradesh, 10, 13, 110, 111
Maharashtra, 87, 109
Malcolm X, 74, 77
Malimath Committee, 100
Mandela, Nelson, 70, 71, 73, 90
Manipur, 101
Marqusee, Mike, 78
Mazar-e-Sharif, 28
Mbeki, Thabo, 72, 73
McNaughton, John, 30–31
media: alternative, 4–5, 66;
corporate influence over, 3–4,
55–59, 83–85, 104;
corporations, 3–4, 33, 43, 58,
66, 83–85; crisis reporting, 2,
6–9, 13, 15–20, 41, 92; critique
of, 1–2, 3–8, 15–16, 19–20,
35–36, 43; distortions, 18–20,
27–29, 57–58; economic and
social aspects, 1–2, 7, 14, 16, 84,
102; Iraq war and, 23–24,
26–29, 33, 47–48, 50, 58;
nations outside US, 1–3, 15–16,
27–29, 35, 101; outlets, 1–5, 15,
24, 43, 57–58; politics and, 2–3,
6–7, 16–17, 57–58, 58–59, 106;
polls, 24, 43, 53; propaganda, 4,
27–28, 35, 37–38, 67, 114–15;
US, 2, 3, 27, 33, 35, 57; war
reporting, 23–24, 27–29, 33,
35–36, 50, 58. *See also* television
Mehndi Kheda, 10, 110

Index

Index

against, 8, 80, 96, 101
Sikligar, Liversingh Tej Singh,
143n12 (99)
da Silva, Luiz Inácio Lula, 90
Singh, Manmohan, 108
slavery, 70, 81
South Africa, 55–56, 64, 71–73, 90
Spain, 53–54
starvation. *See* famine
state: fascism and, 106;
globalization and, 20, 105;
protestors vs., 8, 10–12, 18;
repression by, 12, 16–17, 85–86,
98, 105–7, 110; social services,
20, 106; violence and, 70–71,
85–86, 99–101, 106–7, 112. *See
also* courts; democracy; law;
police
Sunni Muslims, 51

T

Taliban, 48, 51
Tamil Nadu, 98
television: corporate influence over,
2, 57; in Iraq War, 27–29, 44,
48; politics and, 41, 50–51; in
US, 23, 33–35, 48, 58, 64, 74; in
other nations, 27, 57, 103. *See
also* media
terrorism: accusations and opinions
about, 12, 24, 43, 96–99,
143n12; Al-Qaeda, 24, 43; Bush
on, 51–52, 65, 129n33 (38),
130n11(46); causes, 12–13, 86;
ethnic groups and, 99, 143n12;
government response to, 27–28,
63–64, 99; Saddam Hussein and,
24, 43; in India, 96–100,
143n12; laws against, 62–63, 65,

98–100, 103; September 11
attacks, 2, 18, 24, 43, 97; US
and, 38, 62–64, 129n33. *See also*
POTA
Thanksgiving (US), 87–88
Times of India, 143n12
Titanic, 20–21
Togadia, Pravin, 85–86
Tripura, 101
Turkey, 53
turkey pardoning, 87–88

U

Umergaon, 110
United Kingdom (UK). *See* Great
Britain
United Nations (UN): human
rights and, 111; Iraq and, 25, 32,
52–53, 76, 88–89; US and, 29,
39, 47, 76
United States: democracy, 38, 55,
59, 62–63, 67; dictators
supported by, 38, 45–46, 93;
economy, 33–34, 59, 61–63, 66,
84, 89; education, 59–60, 74;
empire, 34, 39, 42–47, 53,
66–67, 83–84, 94; Iraq
intervention (1963), 45; Iraq
occupation, 5, 76, 80–81, 93–94,
132n26; Iraq reconstruction, 32,
63–64; Iraq war and, 43, 59, 76,
97; legal system, 49, 59; media,
2, 3, 27, 33, 35, 57; military
aggression by, 45–47, 65–66, 74,
80, 85–86, 92–93, 97; military
forces, 23–24, 51, 59–60, 74–75,
126n3, 132n26; military
strategies and weapons, 5,
30–31, 35, 44, 52, 84;

155

nationalism in, 37, 52, 67;
Patriot Act, 62–63, 65; politics,
37–38, 47, 51–52, 59, 61–62, 65;
racism in, 36, 59–61, 75;
religious attitudes, 47, 131n13;
resistance movements, 33–34,
36–38, 67–68; terrorism and, 29,
38, 62–63, 64; UN and, 29, 32,
39, 47, 76; Vietnam War, 30–31,
36–37, 74–75, 77
United States Agency for
International Development
(USAID), 64
University of Michigan, 60–61
Untouchables. *See* Adivasis; Dalits
Uttar Pradesh, 98, 111

V

Vajpayee, A.B., 106–7, 112
Viacom, 58
Vietnam War, 30–31, 36–37,
74–75, 77
Vincennes (US navy ship), 42
violence: Hindu and Muslim,
70–71, 80, 85, 96–101, 106–9; in
India, 2–3, 8–12, 81, 94–97, 101,
107–11; in Kashmir, 3, 85,
94–96; by police, 8–12, 18, 81,
110, 142n4; against Sikhs, 80;
state involvement in, 70–71, 85,
96, 100–101, 106; against
women, 8–9, 70, 80, 89, 106,
126n3
Vishwa Hindu Parishad (VHP), 97,
110

W

Wall Street Journal, 63

war: costs of, 32–33, 63; crimes, 46;
democracy and, 53–54, 63;
environmental impacts, 76; legal
issues, 50, 53–54; strategies, 38,
52; weapons of mass destruction,
34–35, 44. *See also* Gulf War; Iraq
war; Vietnam War
War Against Terror, 12, 34, 51–52,
86, 111
water management, 14, 15, 80. *See
also* dams
Water Resources Sector Strategy (World
Bank), 15
Watkin, Kevin, 64
women: in Afghanistan, 50; law
and, 49; violence against, 8–9,
70, 80, 89, 106, 126n3
workers, 10–11, 13, 19, 64, 79–81,
86
Workers' Party (Brazil), 90
World Bank, 15
World Social Forum (WSF), 83,
90–91, 94
World Trade Center, 2, 18, 24, 43,
97
World Trade Organization (WTO),
88–90
World War II, 101
Wyanad, Kerala, 10

ABOUT ARUNDHATI ROY

Arundhati Roy is the author of the novel *The God of Small Things,* for which she was awarded the Booker Prize in 1997. She has also published three essay collections: *War Talk, Power Politics,* and *The Cost of Living,* and is the subject of *The Checkbook and the Cruise Missile: Conversations with Arundhati Roy,* by David Barsamian.
Roy is the recipient of the 2002 Lannan Award for Cultural Freedom from the Lannan Foundation. She was trained as an architect and lives in New Delhi, India.

ABOUT SOUTH END PRESS

South End Press is a nonprofit, collectively run book publisher with more than 250 titles in print. Since our founding in 1977, we have tried to meet the needs of readers who are exploring, or are already committed to, the politics of radical social change. Our goal is to publish books that encourage critical thinking and constructive action on the key political, cultural, social, economic, and ecological issues shaping life in the United States and in the world. In this way, we hope to provide a forum for a wide variety of democratic social movements, and provide an alternative to the products of corporate publishing.

From its inception, the Press has organized itself as an egalitarian collective with decision-making arranged to share as equally as possible the rewards and stresses of running the business. Each collective member is responsible for core editorial and administrative tasks, and all collective members earn the same base salary. The Press also has made a practice of inverting the pervasive racial and gender hierarchies in traditional publishing houses; our staff has had a female majority since the mid-1980s, and has included at least 50 percent people of color since the mid-1990s. Our author list—which includes Arundhati Roy, Noam Chomsky, bell hooks, Winona

LaDuke, Manning Marable, Ward Churchill, Cherríe Moraga, and Howard Zinn—reflects the Press's commitment to publish on diverse issues from diverse perspectives.

To expand access to information and critical analysis, South End Press has been instrumental to the start of two on-going political media projects—Speak Out and *Z Magazine*. We have worked closely with a number of important media and research institutions including Alternative Radio, Political Research Associates, and the Committee on Women, Population and the Environment.

For a free catalog or to order books, you may write to our editorial office: 7 Brookline Street, Cambridge, MA 02139, or visit our website: www.southendpress.org. The website offers the most extensive information on our titles, as well as information on author events, important news, and other interesting links.

Related titles from South End Press

The Checkbook and the Cruise Missile: Conversations with Arundhati Roy
  by David Barsamian

War Talk
  by Arundhati Roy

Power Politics
  by Arundhati Roy